DOGMATIC

Also by Joe Bennett

Just Walking the Dogs (Hazard Press)
Sleeping Dogs and Other Lies (Hazard Press)
Fun Run and Other Oxymorons (Scribner UK)
So Help Me Dog (Hazard Press)
Sit (Hazard Press)
Bedside Lovers (and Other Goats) (Scribner UK)
Doggone (Hazard Press)
Barking (Hazard Press)
A Land of Two Halves (Simon & Schuster UK)
Unmuzzled (Hazard Press)

DOGMATIC

JOE BENNETT

HAZARD PRESS
publishers

The columns that make up this collection first appeared in the *Press*, the *Dominion Post*, the *Otago Daily Times*, the *Southland Times*, the *Waikato Daily Times* and *Hawke's Bay Today*.

Published by Hazard Press
P.O. Box 2151, Christchurch, New Zealand
www.hazardpress.com

First published 2005
Copyright © 2005 Joe Bennett

ISBN   1-877393-11-8

Front cover photograph by C.K. Baker

Printed in New Zealand

Contents

Balloooooooon

I flew to Rotorua to speak at a breakfast function. I arrived the afternoon before. My hosts met me at the airport and said come this way. I thought I would get drinks. I got Christmas decorations. We had to titivate the breakfast room. I was put in charge of blowing up balloons.

It must be ten years since I blew and tied a balloon, and thirty since I did so with any frequency. But like knotting a tie or skiing it proved to be a skill you never lose. As I gripped the little rubber nozzle between finger and thumb and sealed my lips around the little rubber rim, I was flung back through time as if down one of those corny swirling tunnels in a bad science fiction film. Everything was familiar, from the taste and smell and texture of the rubber, to the sense of imminent gaiety.

The only hard breath is the first breath. Sausage balloons in particular can be obstinate, remaining the size of peapods while your cheeks turn the colour of bruises and your eyeballs bulge. But these were round balloons, and round balloons are easy.

The balloon stiffens, momentarily resists, then suddenly, gratifyingly swells before your nose like an out-of-focus vegetable. And with it comes a noise, a sort of one-way roar like a distant engine. That noise says fun to come.

As the rubber stretches, its colour thins from rich to pale, from ruby to pink, from National Party blue to thin spring sky.

You pinch the nozzle to trap the air and you hold the half-inflated balloon in front of you. It's a breast, rounded by the laws of physics and tipped with a nipple, a protuberance of still-dense colour. The flesh yields easily to the touch, moulding, not taut.

A few more breaths and the breast is a pregnancy, hugely swollen, tautly burstable, belly-buttoned and exciting. As the thing grows to block your vision it is tempting to bail out early. You must not bail out early. You must blow that critical extra breath, the one that makes the pregnancy grow a stem, turning a sphere into a pear. It's the peak of inflation and like all peaks it's the moment of greatest danger. You have to judge the exact point between not enough and too much. Not enough and the thing is never a true balloon. It is too small, too dense, a fraction too heavy. Too much and suddenly there's no balloon, only shocked nerves and laughter and a scattering of damp rubber. It's the thrilling razor-edge of harmless peril.

Get it right, get the pear when it's ripe, and a balloon's a rich fat thing. You take it from your mouth and grip it lightly between your thighs. It squeaks like a shoe-sole on linoleum. As you loop the nozzle round and through itself to seal it, sometimes it slips from the fingers and, hey presto, a flying fart. The fart does momentary random loop-the-loops, belching hilarity, and then it's down, floored, scuppered, limp and silent.

You laugh and pick it up again. It's warm. You reinflate it, more easily now that the rubber is stretched and dimpled. You clutch it a tad more tightly between the thighs, tie the knot, pull it tight and then just let it go. What you've made is a wonder. It almost floats. It doesn't fall. It drifts. It's captive happiness. It's impossible to resist batting it.

When you bat it it goes ping, a unique noise, a noise of childhood. It goes away when batted, but slowly and not far. It wants to play.

It begs for a game. It stirs the infant self.

Gravity has hauled at your flesh for years, has slowed you down, withered and bent you, made you ugly. But gravity only grazes a balloon. It's crockery you can drop without consequences. It's a world made soft and pointless, a cartoon world.

A balloon's an equaliser. Everyone's a superstar soccer player, one who can keep the ball aloft with head and shoulder and chest and heel for minutes on end. The cruel rules are in suspension. You're close to the weightless moon of playtime.

Be gentle, says the balloon, wait, I shall come down. And if, as it sinks in its own good gentle time, you swing a real-time foot with real-time venom and volley the balloon with all your muscle-swung might, it scoffs. It goes perhaps a yard at speed, then slows and drifts again, ridiculously soon. It's held and fragile, as temporary as happiness and as good.

Balloons either burst or seep. The held air scatters or leaks. Balloons aren't built to last. They aren't possessable. They exist in the present tense, for fun now, while you can.

The organisers of the breakfast were all as old as I or older, with warts and worries and doctor's appointments. But as the balloons were blown and tied we waded through them laughing at their rulelessness and playing pointless games and being children, now.

The breakfast was okay. But the balloons were better.

Glossy lala

I don't know whether it was an advertising stunt or an accident or a threat but someone left a pornographic magazine in my letterbox. It's as glossy as a yacht and the weight of a paving slab. Rolled up it could be issued to the riot squad. But it's what's inside that's so devastating.

I am not easily shocked but I was shocked. I can only give thanks that I got to it before the local kiddiwinks did. If freedom of speech dictates that such stuff must be published it should at least be sold under brown paper covers and only to adults with a certificate signed by three psychologists testifying to the purchaser's imperturbable mental stability. The magazine in question is the Christmas issue of House and Garden.

The cover features a festive board – yes, that's the sort of language we're dealing with here – groaning – of course – under bowls of soup with swirls of cream in them, glasses of fresh-poured bubbly, lit green candles in a decorative candelabrum beneath a decorative chandelier and beside a decorative centrepiece of Christmas lilies and I don't know what else because I had to avert my eyes. In the background are chairs festooned with cushions, cushions so winsome that I felt the catch in the throat that warns of trouble to come.

I should never have read the text on the cover. I read the text on the cover. Here it is in full: 'Gorgeous table tops. Deck your halls (I am not making this up). Angels and tiaras. (No, really, I am not making this up.) Perfect puddings. Wrap it in an heirloom.'

And inside, well it was everything you could expect and worse. And where do I begin? I shall begin with the prurient glimpses into other people's houses. Either this stuff is all fictional, the people and the places they live in entirely knocked up for the purposes of selling magazines, or else there are two varieties of human beings, two varieties that have diverged so radically by the process of evolution that they can barely recognise each other, and I belong to the other variety. Here is a world where beds are made, pillows creaseless and 'in Wendy's wardrobe European shoes are lined up with military precision'. There's even a photograph of the wardrobe and the shoes, pair after pair of them, flimsy as tissue paper, barely capable of supporting the weight of their price tags.

It's a strange and horrible world to which they recruit them young. Tots design their own awful bedrooms. 'Six-year-old Iona has a green and cream toile wallpaper, matching curtains and upholstered slipper chair (slipper chair!) and an old French wooden bed. Georgia, almost twelve,…has a sophisticated tented ceiling. (What's sophisticated about it is left unsaid. The word itself just stamps its own unarguable assertion. It's sophisticated because it's sophisticated.) Olivia, fourteen, relaxes on her "four-poster" achieved mainly with fabric.' It's all there in that last sentence. In House-and-Garden Land cloth is never cloth, nor is it even material. It is always fabric. And Olivia, poor thing, is not relaxing. She is posing for the camera on the 'four-poster' with a dog. Appearances suggest that if Fido were to leap onto the 'four-poster' at any time other than when the House and Garden photographer was present it would be sent forthwith to the dog shelter. And the moment the snap was taken, of course, the dog ran off in search of things to kill, eat or roll in and so, if she's got any sense, did Olivia.

Otherwise she's doomed to a life in which 'organic textures, flavours and fragrances set the scene for Christmas in a marquee. Coco husks sprinkled underfoot scent the air with chocolate. A bird bath and terracotta planters sprayed with copper act as centrepieces, encircled with bay leaves and cinnamon sticks and holding branches of twisted willow or reeds and dried orange slices.'

It's all there in sumptuous colour photography, the table ware arrayed around the copper-sprayed bird bath and the dried orange slices. The glasses and napery are set just so. No shots of the aftermath, of course, no candid snaps of stacked and sullied crockery, or of the live-in Filipina treasure with the chapped hands bent over the scullery sink, or of Uncle Trevor drunk as a moose in rut. No record either of the conversation that took place around the copper-sprayed bird bath over the cloying fragrance (no smells allowed in paradise) of the crushed coco husks. Imagine that conversation. On second thoughts, don't bother. Spare yourself. The conversation is irrelevant. It didn't happen. For this is lala-land.

Most telling of all, as you flick through the magazine it's impossible, at a glance, to distinguish the text from the ads. Both picture the perfect, the faultless, the moment before things happen, the moment of expectation, of order, of hope, of idealised material lust, of how things should be but aren't. It's porn.

Badlands revisited

It had been five long years and three medium-length ones since Pete and I last journeyed to the Land of Cliché. We suffered wounds on that trip but by now we'd got them licked. It was time to return. We yearned to see for ourselves the fabled Vale of Bed-linen where all was soft and lovely. And this time we went prepared. We took with us a cook-cum-bodyguard in the form of a South African rugby player. Six foot six in his stockinged feet, a black belt in ju-jitsu, a green belt in town planning and a former top-flight chef with South African Airways, he was one out of the Boks. We could rely on him to do the hard yards, leaving Pete and me the squidgy ones.

This time we chose to travel by water. The choice of boat I left to the Bok.

'Canoe?' he said.

'I can,' I said, so that was settled. Pausing only to tell the Bok to remove his stockings, we set off, paddling up the River Yonder against the tide of public opinion. But this was not the calm brown Yonder of which you hear so little. No, we were paddling that sky-coloured turbulence, famed and feared the length and breadth and height of Cliché Land, the barely navigable wild blue Yonder. It churned like a washing machine and put us through the wringer.

The Bok proved a disappointment, sitting with his feet over the gunwales while we did all the work. When I told him to get paddling he showed me a clean pair of heels. 'Put your stockings back on,' I said from the back of the canoe, sternly, 'and pull your socks up. We've got work to do. This is serious.'

'Make me,' said the Bok.

From my bag of provisions I pulled a coil of copper wire and a magnet. The effect was electric. The Bok started paddling like a madman. A madman who happened to be passing looked on in admiration.

'Keep an eye on that man,' I whispered to Pete, 'I don't trust him.' Pete knitted his brow and crocheted an eye which he attached to the Bok.

'You're crazy,' said the Bok, 'you'll never make it. No one goes to the Land of Cliché and comes back in one piece.' But with Pete's eye on him he could get up to no mischief.

Then suddenly a giant wave flung us around and the boat was facing the wrong way. We struggled to turn it back but it was no use.

Pete stated the obvious. 'The obvious,' he said. 'From now on we'll have to do the journey in reverse.'

'You mean,' I said, my jaw dropping.

'Yes,' said Pete, 'we'll have to go backwards going forward.'

Pete's face was a rictus of effort, his lips stretched across his teeth. Reinserting my jaw I asked Pete how long he thought we could keep going like this, but he remained tight-lipped. Fear was written on his face. Terror was scrawled on his neck. Pete was never hard to read.

'How far to Bed-linen?' I asked the Bok.

'Search me,' he said. I did, but I found only a couple of lumps of biltong. Then suddenly, with a terrible groaning that I shall never forget as long as I remember it, the mountain in front of us swelled at the base and narrowed at the top. So did the trees on Yonder bank.

'My God,' screamed Pete. 'It's all going pear-shaped.'

'Ha ha,' said the Bok, a grim leer playing about his features and hopping over to Pete to play about his. 'Pear-shaped's not the half of it. This is a paradigm shift.'

'What's a paradigm shift?' I screamed above the noise.

'Nobody knows,' said the Bok, 'but boy, does it sound impressive.'

'I'll get us out of this,' said Pete, gritting his teeth. Spitting grit as he went, he single-handedly held the canoe steady against the raging waters. When he applied his other hand we inched forward backwards, turned a bend and found ourselves in the fabled Vale of Bed-linen.

But all was not soft and lovely. Wet manchester hung from the trees and slapped horribly at our faces as we paddled past. And then to make things worse the heavens opened and from them poured a cascade of eggs, milk and sugar, turning the stream beneath our hull to a turbid sweetness that threatened to engulf us. It wrenched the paddle from Pete's hands. When a small branch floated past, I twigged. This wasn't the fabled Vale of Bed-linen. This was Sheet Creek, we were up it without a paddle, and it was all turning to custard.

Grammar with teeth

I taught for twenty years. Now I'm doing it again, part time for a month or two. Nothing's changed. I stand in front of classes and I try to interest them in words. I speak of nouns and verbs and how they reflect the world. I praise the power of simplicity. I say that language is thought, that language is what separates us from the beasts, that shoddy language is a crime. I rant and I clown and I sweat but it doesn't seem to do much good. Most pupils just wait for time to pass. They want to be away and doing. I often think I'm wasting my time. I can rely on only one person to be interested and it seems absurd to drive all the way to school in order to interest myself.

Education is a curious business. And today on this heavy summer Sunday I was going to write about it. I wanted to detail the folly of the NCEA and the bankruptcy of educational theory and the misconception of the nature of the child. I would use a lot of abstract nouns. My tone would be earnest and adult. But then the puppy arrived. I had agreed to look after it for the day. The puppy put paid to earnest and adult.

When people buy a puppy they see it as a bundle of adjectives. That snub little muzzle is cute. That tottering run is endearing. Those big brown eyes are adorable. But the buyer soon discovers that the adjectives are only a sales pitch. A puppy isn't adjectives. A puppy's a verb. It does stuff. And it learns by doing stuff. For a puppy, to be and to do and to learn are the same verb.

I looked after the puppy for eight hours. During those eight hours it stopped being a verb for approximately five minutes. Those five minutes happened to coincide with the five minutes that I was being a verb. I was restraining the puppy.

A puppy is crammed with vitality. Inside its tiny frame I could feel the verbs squirming. Restraining it was like trying to hold a bag of corks under water.

Abstract nouns don't interest a puppy. Nouns such as education or language or thought are no good because they can't be bitten. What a puppy wants are concrete nouns and this puppy found concrete nouns all over my house. And having found them it bit them in order to learn what they would do.

The shoe didn't do a lot but it tasted faintly of cow. Cow is meat. Meat is food. The puppy chewed the shoe until I got up from the computer and did a verb, whereupon the puppy transferred its attention to another concrete noun. This noun is twelve years old and called Jessie. Jessie is experienced in the ways of puppies. She's a good teacher. The puppy nipped her. Jessie growled. The puppy stood back a moment to absorb the lesson and then decided not to. It nipped her again. Jessie snapped the air an inch from the puppy's nose. This time the puppy absorbed the lesson. But the lesson it absorbed was specific rather than general. The puppy learned not to bite this particular concrete noun. But it didn't learn not to bite all concrete nouns of the same class.

Another concrete noun of the same class was lying on the sofa. His name is Baz. Baz is not experienced in the ways of puppies. He is three years old, 35 kilos, as fit as an orchestra of fiddles and a great killer of possums. The puppy was roughly the size of a possum.

The puppy leapt onto the sofa and bit Baz's ear. Baz did nothing. The puppy bit his cheek. Baz tried to shake the puppy off. The puppy held on. Baz sighed and got off the sofa with the puppy hanging from his cheek like a toothed pendant. I have known several teachers like Baz.

Baz lay down. The puppy was delighted. It discovered a world of prepositions. It walked around Baz and burrowed under him and jumped onto him and clambered over him and bit into him.

To distract the puppy and to rescue Baz I led them into the garden and turned on the hose. The puppy let go of Baz in order to bite the stream of water. But the water acted more like a verb than a noun. It refused to stay bitten. The hose proved a far more satisfactory noun. And then the puppy saw the chooks. Here was food on the move. Here were nouns that did stuff. Suddenly there were verbs everywhere: run, chase, scatter, bark, squawk, fly. I contributed a few verbs myself. Bellow was the first of them, followed by pursue, lunge, miss, slip, fall and swear. The puppy loved it.

And so it went on. The cat was met and barked at. A milk carton was chased and seized and thrown and chased again. And whenever things grew dull there was always Baz to assault. The puppy met a multitude of nouns and committed a multitude of verbs. It learned a lot and it was happier than any kid in school. And all without a word. It was an education.

Dig this

The dogs did better than I did at Christmas. I got a CD of carols. The dogs each got a synthetic chicken leg made from what looked like green concrete. I consoled myself with a couple of whitebait.

I caught the whitebait in a local stream, fell for them and determined to keep them as pets. But my aquarium was full of goldfish and I suspected that goldfish would approach whitebait in the same way as people do. So I built the goldfish a pond.

According to a discouraging booklet that I made the mistake of reading, nature abhors a pond. Nature wants to render every pond stagnant, clog it with sludge, kill all aquatic creatures, replace those creatures with plants, replace the plants with trees, then crack open a bottle of bubbly and announce that there's another pond gone. The process may take a while but nature is famously patient.

At the same time, according to the booklet, a garden pond is simple to make. All you need is a sheet of industrial grade plastic, and a strong back for digging. I had a sheet of industrial grade plastic.

I thought of playing the CD of carols to encourage me as I dug. But the carols turned out to be New Zealand carols which are different from ordinary carols in that they're horrible. They substitute pohutukawa for holly, and possums for reindeer. I don't know why. The southern hemisphere seems to me the ideal place to start the revolution of honesty. Instead of adapting distant spiritual self-delusion into local spiritual self-delusion, we should ditch the lot and rechristen Christmas Shoppingmas. And no, I don't think it will happen either.

I left the CD on my desk and set to work. Digging through topsoil is an easy pleasure and I swiftly shifted both inches of it before an audience of a cat, a pair of dogs and six chickens who didn't seem to mind that the dogs were chewing on synthetic chicken legs. Beneath the topsoil lay clay. Digging through clay is not an easy pleasure. Nor is it digging. It is shaving. By lunchtime I had a depression, by afternoon tea a holelet, and by dinner time a bad back. I slept on it.

Sleep did nothing for the back but it did wonders for the holelet. It turned it back into a depression. Chooks adore freshly dug soil. Indeed the only thing they adore more than freshly dug soil, is scratching freshly dug soil back into where it was freshly dug from. But at least, as I redug my holelet in the morning, I was now working to the tuneful accompaniment of my spine.

I also had less digging to do than I'd expected. Rereading the discouraging booklet in bed I had discovered that my pond could only be 400 millimetres deep. 401 millimetres and a government agent on an aerial reconnaissance mission would spot it, radio a message to base, and within minutes a crack squad of enforcement officers, armed to the gills with forms in triplicate, would descend and instruct me that the law required a 9-foot fence of razor wire round my pond to prevent the toddlers of Lyttelton from committing collective hara-kiri in my pond like so many chubby lemmings. I dug to a depth of 399 millimetres. The mothers of Lyttelton can breathe easy.

A sheet of polythene fits into a hole in the same way as a sheet of pastry doesn't fit into a pie dish. Both form pleats. With pastry a judicious thumb can squidge the pleats into the wall. With polythene a judicious thumb can't, but it can turn on a garden hose. Remarkably my pleated pond filled up with water. Even more remarkably it didn't appear to leak. The cat, the chooks and I stood back to watch. The dogs stepped in to watch.

I tipped sand round the dogs to form a bed. The water turned the colour of tea. Undeterred I drove to a local pond that nature hadn't yet got round to abhorring nor the government to fencing, and collected weed, tadpoles and an abundance of insects. Back home I tipped everything into the tea-coloured water and followed it with the goldfish. The tea drank the lot.

Then I tipped the whitebait into the vacated aquarium and sat at my desk with a cigarette to watch them. Within five minutes the whitebait were as happy as a dog with a synthetic chicken leg. And so was I. I fell into a reverie of gazing in much the same way as a child falls into an unfenced pond.

A smell roused me. It was the smell of plastic burning. I looked out the window. To my astonishment the pool had not caught fire. But the CD of carols I had placed beside the ashtray was smouldering nicely. I'd have liked to think it was an act of god, but the evidence suggested otherwise in the form of a cigarette absent-mindedly stubbed out on track three.

In sum, then, I'd had a Christmas of firsts. I'd acquired my first pet whitebait, built my first pond and burned my first CD.

Pap

I thought for a moment I'd found hope. In the paper last Thursday, just above the story of the sixty-three-year-old Pole who went to hospital complaining of headaches, there was a story about the Queen.

The Queen was hosting a reception for representatives of the British music industry. If I'd been the Queen I'd have pretended to have a headache and joined the Pole in hospital, but the Queen is a better woman than I am. She stayed at home and did her horrible duty. And there's a picture of her doing it.

She is immediately recognisable. She is wearing a standard-issue Queen dress the colour of seasickness. The hemline stands where it has always stood on the Queen, which is there, right there, and not an eighth of an inch either way. The hair, too, is as it's always been, a sort of lacquered motor bike helmet, grey with years of meeting representatives of music industries, but still recognisably the Queen's hair.

Ranged before the Queen are three famous men. There's Jimmy Page of Led Zeppelin, Brian May of Queen, and Mr Eric Clapton. They are standing in attitudes of deference and Mr Clapton is delicately shaking hands with the Queen and bowing from the hips. Despite their fame, however, none of these men is immediately recognisable, for each is wearing a suit. They are not known for wearing suits. They made their names wearing the opposite of suits. They wore jeans and young-person clothes, clothes that announced they were ordinary people, like you or me, and not part of the nasty establishment that repressed ordinary people and kept us away from the power and wealth and fame that were rightfully ours.

If thirty years ago you had shown these musicians a snap of themselves dressed like bankers and deferring to royalty, they would have scoffed. They stood in counterpoint to all that stuff.

And throughout those thirty years, while they shinned up the ladder of success in their jeans, the Queen's just carried on carrying on, lacquering her hair, retaining her hemline and shaking deferential hands. It was the musicians who moved away from her unchanging world and now they have come back to it, speaking politely. I find that ironic, but it's not what gave me the sniff of hope.

The musicians have made a lot of music. Some of it is tuneful but all of it is pap. And I resent it. It is not the pappiness that I resent. There has always been and will always be an abundance of pap in the world and resenting it is like resenting oxygen or lust. What I resent is that this pap has slithered into my skull.

I can hum tunes by Eric Clapton. I can recite lyrics by Queen with only minor inaccuracies. I don't want to. I didn't ask any of it in. It has just occupied the air for all forty-seven years of my life, assaulting me from radios and in lifts and while I have waited for people in suits to answer the telephone. Everywhere I've been, that same music has been too. There is no escaping it.

Unless, that is, you're the Queen. For it was words the Queen spoke that gave me my momentary flutter of hope. As Eric Clapton, the erstwhile youngster, bowed his head and clasped her hand and spoke sweet conventional emptinesses, the Queen apparently said to him, to the universally celebrated Mr Clapton, 'And what exactly do you do?'

I wish I'd been there. I'd have cheered. Cheered at the thought that it might just be possible to escape the universal pap, the musical candyfloss, the shallow emotive background to our shallow emotive lives.

But it can't be done. Unless you're a Queen who lives in rarefied abstraction, the pap gets you in the end. It lodges in the skull and wears you down. If it were possible to buy a cranial vacuum cleaner and suck out all the Eric Clapton pap and the Beatles pap and the Elton Bloody John pap and all the inane rest of it that I've absorbed simply by being alive, I'd be down at Betta Electrical before you could say yellow submarine. But it isn't. The stuff will stay in my head till I keel over. And what's especially cruel it that it will probably stay there when the good stuff starts to leak out.

There I'll be, twenty years from now on a sunny Wednesday afternoon, wedged in a floral armchair in the lounge of the Eventide Home for Withered Hacks, and some well-meaning young thing will breeze in all cheery cheery and sit down at the piano and bash out a whole string of those appalling tunes in the hope that we husks will feel a ghost of a sap-rise and will remember when the world was young. And I'll probably sing along. Oh God. There is no hope.

Except that is for the Pole with the headaches. Apparently the doctors found a 12-centimetre knife blade buried in his skull. They removed it without difficulty. The Pole said he'd probably acquired the knife when he came home drunk and fell off a kitchen stool. Nothing wrong with that of course, but I don't believe him. I suspect he was trying to dig the tunes out.

Against

It is rare for George Bush and me to have anything in common beyond a similar number of limbs. But right now we're both at war.

George says he's fighting a war against terror. That's an obvious nonsense. You can't fight terror. Emotions don't emerge to do battle. George's war is unwinnable.

My war's unwinnable too, but it's a lot more fun. I'm fighting thistles. And I've got a new weapon. It's a pump-action backpack. I love it. I fill it with 15 litres of water and a teaspoon of expensive chemistry. Then I put my arms through the straps and hoist the thing onto my spine. If I slipped a jerkin over the top I'd look like Quasimodo. But I don't care. When you're at war, appearance counts for nothing. Only killing counts.

Ted Hughes got it right about thistles. 'Against the rubber tongues of cows,' he wrote, 'and the hoeing hands of men, thistles spike the summer air.'

All seventeen of those words are bang-right, but one is the bang-rightest of all. That word is 'against'. Thistles are against. And I'm against thistles.

They are vegetable warriors. They have no friends. They do no good. They exist simply to fight for empire. If we let them they'd overrun the world.

The moment that winter wanes, thistles spring. They grow as you watch, recolonising last year's land and making a grab for more. They stab the sky in mute aggression. They are malice with roots. You get the sense that those roots frustrate them. Thistles would like to be up and doing, wandering the land, spiking things, buggering things up.

When out on the hills with the dogs I sometimes stop for a spot of communion with the sky and the land and the sea and a cigarette. I sit on the grass and a small thistle surprises my buttocks. I rise like a startled quail.

But it's not these thistles that offend me most, nor yet the Scottish-looking ones that grow as tall as my ribs and sprout a flower like a centurion's plume. The thistles I'm at war with are the crinklies. Crinklies grow out rather than up. Their prickles are daggers. Their leaves are thick and fleshy and the colour of battleships. And they spread. If left to themselves crinklies will form a bank of ferocity that renders a whole hillside impassable.

My dogs and I have carved our own paths over the hills. Those paths please me. They remind me of ancient trade routes, threads through the wilderness. Every year the crinklies try to block those paths.

Thistles don't daunt my young dog. He's a dingbat and he doesn't do forethought. He blunders through thistles as he blunders through life, with gusto. But when my old dog comes across a bank of thistles she stops and surveys it, then highsteps around it on dainty toes, her nose wrinkled with distaste. And so do I.

Up until now I have fought the thistles with boot and stick and sometimes long-handled shears. But this year I got serious. I slung 15 litres of herbicide on my back and I went to war.

I was never a student of physics or a fan of the metric system, but I believe that 15 litres of water weighs 15 kilos. Fifteen kilos is plenty.

My friend Fred recently went on a diet and shed 15 kilos. Now when he stands still in the street, dogs cock their legs against him. Fred was understandably keen to illustrate exactly how much weight he'd lost, so he went to the supermarket and loaded his trolley with thirty pats of butter. Halfway to the checkout he realised that this little brag was going to cost him over $60, so he ditched the trolley mid-aisle. (It must have puzzled the employee who eventually came across it. Did he imagine perhaps that someone had had second thoughts about a remake of *Last Tango in Paris?*)

But my point is that 15 kilos is plenty. Fred wore his round the waist where they helped his stability. I wore mine on my back where they didn't.

The hills behind my house are steep. Quasimodo climbed Notre Dame with ease, but Quasimodo didn't have to squirt things with his hump. Nor did he have his hands full. My left hand was operating a lever that pumped the pressure, and my right hand was pointing the hose that dealt death. So when I overbalanced, this left my nose free to break my fall.

I overbalanced repeatedly. I slithered on weeds. I rolled down rocks. I fell into thistles. But I persevered. In war you have no choice. It's kill or surrender.

Even the smallest thistle got a squirt of chemistry. The crinklies got a drenching. That was five days ago. Each day since then I've been back up the hill to gloat. One day and the thistle heads were nodding. Two days, drooping. And now, this sunny morning, whole thistles are wilting delightfully. The stuffing's gone out of them. They're dying. It's a joy. I may lose the war in the end, but for now I appear to be winning. It would make George green with envy.

George wouldn't enjoy feeling envy. He'd probably wage a war against it.

Weather or not

A low foggy morning. Fog had crept into the harbour basin, had swaddled the port in cotton wool.

Some mornings I feel lithe and alive, with teeth, like an eel. But not this morning. This morning I woke with a clogged head, as though the fog had filled it. I had writing to do but the words came heavy and fat and slow.

I drank coffee of course, and from my best mug, one decorated with the cover design of a novel by Evelyn Waugh. Waugh wrote prose as sharp and as clean and as murderous as a scalpel, but my prose refused to clear.

So I went up the hill with the dogs, through air that was summer-warm and graveyard-still and dense with fog. Fog. Even the word sounds clogged with itself, choked.

Fog's a staple of horror movies. Fog always shrouds the castle of the blood-sucking count, and it smothers the river valley where the murderer lurks, because fog makes a known world mysterious.

We can never know what's round the corner, but when fog descends we don't even know if there's a corner. Fog intensifies our ignorance. The world shrinks to here and very close to here. Fog underlines the present tense. Everything else is unknowable.

But what's round the corner still fascinates us and there have always been people to exploit that fascination. First came the woman with the crystal ball and the talk of tall dark strangers, but these days she has any number of rivals vying to corner the future market: zodiac interpreters, tarot touts, quivering mediums, ouija fraudsters and financial advisers, all of them offering to give us a glimpse of the yet-to-come and all of them every bit as befogged as the client.

And then there are the television weather forecasters. Poor things, they've become celebrities, but it's their own fault.

Like any fairground huckster they now start with a tease, popping into the bulletin early on and promising to give us the low-down on who's going to get wet tomorrow and who's going to bask. It's a titillatory bait no different from the fortune teller's come-on line. It's the promise of a sneak preview of the unknown, an insider tip.

Then when they do appear they drag it out. They tell us first what we already know, presenting the weather that's just gone as a form of competition. Today's prize for the highest temperature goes to plucky little Hororata, and Hororata puffs out its chest and endures the insincere applause of the rest of country.

But then comes the meaty stuff, the future. And thanks to the potent engines of science, the satellites, the monitoring stations, the anemometers in Antarctica, they generally get the short-range forecast right. But unlike science they offer it with judgement attached. Rain gets a grim black symbol on the weather map and the presenter puts on the long face of regret. Whereas sunshine gets a merry symbol and a smile-drenched promise that tomorrow will be a lovely day for a picnic on the Port Hills or some other improbable activity drawn from the *Weather Forecaster's Bumper Book of Nice Family Fun*.

In other words the weather forecast appears to be information but in fact it's just a show. A show that tames the unknown. And a show that rests on false assumptions.

The first is the assumption that it is good to know the future. It isn't. Every character in mythology who was granted the gift of foresight ended up in tears.

The second is that we need to know what the weather will be like. Most of us don't. Unless we farm or put to sea in little boats, the weather has little influence over what we do.

The third is that there is good weather and bad weather, kind stuff and cruel. Not so. There is only weather. Without its variety we would all be dead.

And then there is the assumption that we don't like to be surprised. We do like to be surprised. Without surprise there is only boredom.

And so it was this morning, as I lumbered up the hill through the cloud with a head to match. For suddenly, in the space of perhaps 10 yards, I climbed out of the fog and into the summer sun. I stopped and turned and looked. Below me lay a basin of fog, obscuring the town and the port and the water. The fog was a thick-ridged creaminess, like a meringue, seemingly dense enough to walk on. And out of the far side of the fog, the hills of the peninsula rose sharp as cut paper and washed with lemon light.

This is all right, I thought, and I stood to stare, sensing my mind clear as I did so. I came down the hill smiling and keen to work. And if I'd known it was going to be like that it wouldn't have been as good.

Gumdigger

'Pass the Luxator,' said the dentist, and I heard the hygienist open a drawer and rootle through what sounded like a tangle of cutlery.

I didn't see the Luxator because it passed from hygienist to dentist in that area behind the dental chair where worryingly invisible things go on, but I knew what it was going to do. It was going to pull a tooth from my head.

Time was when tooth-pulling was the only sort of dentistry. In the thirteenth century the dentist was the local barber. If, while he was placing the pudding bowl over a customer's scalp in order to deliver the fashionable cut of the day, the customer mentioned that one of his teeth was troubling him, the barber would summon his hygienist. The medieval hygienist was not a young woman with breasts, but rather a grown man with forearms. The barber seized the tooth with forceps while the hygienist seized the patient with determination. The barber pulled, the patient screamed and the hygienist held on.

The only advantage of medieval dentistry was that in the course of your life, even if you suffered from the worst teeth imaginable, you could only go to the dentist thirty-two times. Thereafter you got your haircuts from the gum specialist.

Since then, life and dentistry have evolved in step with each other.

In the thirteenth century both were brief, cheap and painful. Today, by and large, they're both long, expensive and painless.

The only other time I've had a tooth out, the dentist was eighty years old and the tooth about eight. This time both dentist and tooth were in their forties. The tooth was an iceberg, nine-tenths of it hidden below the gum line. Above the gum there was only a battered stump, a stump that had been drilled and shaped and pinned and filled I don't know how many times. Each one of those fillings had been a source of pride and income to the dentist who created it, and a source of tutting and income to the dentist who later replaced it.

But now the tooth was beyond salvage, and the dentist and I had had a mature professional discussion about it along the following lines:

Dentist: I think that tooth should go.

Me: Will you have to use the drill?

Dentist: No.

Me: Will it hurt?

Dentist: No.

Me: I think that tooth should go too.

He delivered the anaesthetic with a highly amusing needle a couple of yards in length, then we waited for my lower lip to sag and fill with saliva as with certain children in the lower streams whom it was always a joy to teach. To fill the time I said I expected that advances in technology meant that modern dentists rarely got to pull a tooth. He replied that, on the contrary, he pulled several every day, especially when there were foreign ships in port.

'The Poles and the Russians just don't look after their teeth,' he said. 'They're also impervious to pain. Half of them can't be bothered with an anaesthetic. But the Koreans are all wimps.'

So saying he prodded my gum a bit, asked if it hurt, then called for the Luxator. Gripping my jaw almost as firmly as I was gripping the arms of the chair, he set to work. I did not know what the Luxator looked like, not could I feel what it was up to, but I imagined it as a sort of space-age miniature vacuum cleaner that would suck the tooth from my jawbone before you could say 'Did I tell you about my Korean heritage?'

Perhaps because the stump was so negligible, the vacuum cleaner took a while to suck. But then there came a graunching sound and a disconcertingly triumphant 'That's got it' from the dentist, and after four merry decades my tooth and I parted company.

'I don't suppose you want to see the tooth,' said the dentist.

He supposed wrong. I am a world-ranked coward but I have never been squeamish. Indeed I take a morbid interest in previously unseen bits of the body. Some years ago one of my dogs was hit by a car. After the operation on his shattered femur the vet showed me a shard of bone that he had been unable to fit back in. I took it home as a grisly souvenir.

As it happened, a couple of days later I showed the bone to the recuperating dog. He sniffed at it, then ate it.

I was not tempted to eat my tooth. It was a sorry thing, discoloured with age and abuse. Far more interesting was the blood-streaked Luxator. It had a worn wooden handle and a grey metal shaft. It certainly wasn't a space-age miniature vacuum cleaner. Indeed it looked like a thirteenth-century screwdriver. The dentist was fingering it with every appearance of affection.

And if I hadn't had a mouth full of blood and cotton wool, and if I hadn't been exploring with my tongue the exciting new gap in my mouth that I shall take to the grave, and if I hadn't been thinking 'one down, thirty-one to go', I'd have asked him to throw in a haircut.

Destiny's children

I'm looking at a picture of Brian Tamaki attending a rally. Mr Tamaki is the spiritual leader of an organisation called Destiny Church. Apparently Mr Tamaki led the rally on an extremely spiritual Harley Davidson motor bike, but sadly the bike is not pictured.

Mr Tamaki is wearing black trousers and a black shirt. Black clothing has a long and splendid spiritual history. Black shirts, for example, have always attracted the sort of people who are spiritually right and keen to mend the ways of the spiritually wrong.

Mr Tamaki is also wearing sunglasses. Sunglasses have a less extensive but still promising spiritual history. In recent years they have been favoured by such spiritual leaders as bouncers, gangsters and New Zealand First MPs. Mr Tamaki may be wishing to express his solidarity with these spiritual leaders, but I wouldn't be surprised if he were also, and typically, thinking of the ordinary people. For eyes are the windows of the soul, and Mr Tamaki's soul is of such sun-like radiance that a glimpse of it would damage any mortal retina.

If you look closely at the picture you can see that the man behind Mr Tamaki is fiddling with an earpiece in the best spiritual tradition of CIA bruisers. It is not clear who is talking into that earpiece but I expect it is God, issuing instructions for the rally held in his name.

The appearance of Mr Tamaki and friends, then, is spiritually promising. But, as any spiritual analyst will tell you, what matters is substance, and I am pleased to report that Mr Tamaki has a lot of substance. Aside from being a strongly built chap he is also a television evangelist. Television evangelists have a long history of spiritual and financial excellence. Admittedly that financial excellence has led some of them into the valley of sin where the prostitutes dwell, but then they've wept and asked for forgiveness and more money. I don't know if Mr Tamaki has done any weeping yet, but he's certainly asked for money. He tells his congregation that they should give money to Destiny churches, because that is what God wants.

According to its poorly spelt but deeply spiritual website, Destiny Church is a 'god-appointed apostolic ministry'. Of the two apostles or 'senior pastors' that God has appointed, one is Mr Tamaki. The other, by an extraordinary coincidence, is Mrs Tamaki. Families don't come any holier.

The rally at which the photo was taken was called to oppose the Civil Union Bill, the bill that will permit dangerous homosexuals to form quasi-marriages that will gnaw at the fabric of society.

God and Mr Tamaki are both opposed to such quasi-marriages. What God wants is always right. Mr Tamaki wants what God wants. Therefore Mr Tamaki is always right too. It's an impressive form of reasoning, known in the business as begging the question.

At the rally, Mr Tamaki's disciples carried placards bearing the legend 'Enough is Enough', which is an example of the same impressive reasoning. It can't be faulted. Enough is indeed enough, just as a circular argument is a circular argument, and a cult is a cult, and inflammatory fundamentalism is inflammatory fundamentalism.

Lots of children took part in the rally but some of them hadn't quite grasped the meaning of 'enough is enough'. When interviewed by a reporter, one child amusingly interpreted the message as meaning 'we're standing up against the bad people'. Children in black shirts have stood up against the bad people before and have proved jolly good at it.

But if some of the children were puzzled, fortunately the Maxim Institute was there to help them. The Maxim Institute kindly wrote a letter explaining to the children what they, the children, thought about the Civil Union Bill. Having found out what they thought, the children could then sign the letter and send it to the nasty government. It turned out, astonishingly, that what the children thought was exactly the same as what the Maxim Institute thought and what Destiny New Zealand thought.

Destiny New Zealand is the political wing of Destiny Church. Churches with political wings have a splendid spiritual record. They've made a lot of history happen. Much of that history has been bloody, but you can hardly blame the churches or the spiritual leaders for that. They've merely been doing God's bidding for the good of society. And if they've had to tickle up a few members of that society in order to impress upon them what a loving God wants of them, then so be it. Over the centuries there have been a wide variety of tickling sticks and they've proved jolly useful. Imagine the mess we'd be in now if it hadn't been for the rack, the thumbscrew, the stake, the gas-chambers, the suicide bombers and all the rest of those expressions of the divine will.

Destiny is a young organisation but it follows a formula that is as old as mankind. It takes its mandate from a mythological authority. It defies reason, brainwashes children and fleeces the weak. There ought to be words to describe a formula so banal yet so persistent and so effective, and there are. The kindest of those words is delusional. The most direct is evil.

Consider the zip

'Strange to be ignorant of the way things work,' wrote dear old dismal Larkin. Larkin was writing about big things like seasons and reproduction but he might as well have been writing about little things. Things like zips.

Consider the zip. I have one in front of me as I write. Nothing strange in that of course. Like most men I normally have a zip in front of me. Indeed I often have several zips in front of me. When dog-walking I wear a vest that consists almost entirely of zips. There's a zip pocket for the leads, another for cigarettes, another for plastic bags in case someone's watching, and yet another for pieces of dried ox liver with which to bribe the dogs. That jacket and I have done thousands of miles and probably a hundred ox livers. It's a fine and fragrant thing.

But that jacket's by no means my sum total of zips. I own bags with zips and cushions with zips and duvet covers with zips and several of those natty little plastic files with zips. For a recent journey I even bought two pairs of those young person trousers that are more zip than trouser. And of course all my conventional trousers, bar one, have a zip. The exception is the trousers that go with my ancient dinner jacket. Those trousers have a button fly. Over a couple of decades of dress-up functions I have discovered that the ease of operating a button fly is inversely proportional to the urgency of the situation.

Indeed I wouldn't be in the least surprised to learn that in 1893 it was a button fly and a situation of urgency that induced Mr Yashid Khaled Kuzorski of New York to invent, perfect and patent the zip fastener. Then all he had to do was to sit back and wait for the world to beat a path to his door. It did and it continues to do so for the zip is a simple, practical and efficient thing. I can even forgive Mr Kuzorski for stamping his initials on his zips.

But the zip in front of me is no longer efficient. It's the zip down the front of my dog-walking vest and this morning I went to do it up and nothing happened. The zip fastener was stuck fast. So I did the sensible thing and tried to force it. No joy.

I extracted the little thingy from the slot and studied it. It seemed fine. The slot did too, so I reunited them and tried again. And again and again and again. In dog training this is known as an extinction burst.

Let's say, for example, that whenever your dog scratches at the door you let the dog in. The dog has learnt that scratching the door opens it. Then one day the dog scratches at the door and you don't let the dog in, perhaps because you are trying to mend a zip. Does the dog rationalise the situation and say, 'Ah well, scratching doesn't work any more, I suppose I'll have to try turning the handle'? No, it scratches the door harder.

Flies do something similar. They headbut closed windows. And even though there's an open window right alongside, they carry on headbutting the closed one until you either open the window or swat the fly. If you open the window, the fly has learnt that headbutting works. If you swat the fly, well, it's beyond learning. And mention of flies takes me back to the zip.

As I say I repeatedly tried to zip the zip but without success. My extinction burst led eventually to extinction and I brought the thing home unzipped and I laid it on my desk and I studied it.

A zip consists of two ranks of teeth and a thing shaped like a goblet. The ranks of teeth feed separately into the mouth of the goblet and then emerge from its base fused. And for the life of me I can't see how. Without the goblet it is impossible to fuse the teeth. I've tried. I've tried jamming them together. I've tried laying them on top of each other and pressing them together. And yet the goblet appears to be nothing more than, well, a goblet. I've studied the thing with a magnifying glass. And what have I learnt? Zip. Or rather I have learnt that I don't understand how zips work and I would never have invented them.

And in the light of that realisation I look around my study. I see paper. I do not know how to make paper. Plastic, ditto; glass, ditto; metal, ditto; a ballpoint pen, ditto; and as for a telephone or a computer or a printer, ditto in excelsis. If a nuclear blast were to demolish civilisation I'd be the guy sitting whimpering amid the rubble with no idea how to start again. Strange to be ignorant of the way things work indeed, strange and helpless. I shall go to my grave in ignorance, and, unlike Mr Kuzorski, I shall go to that grave without ever having had the wit to invent anything. Unless, that is, you count names like Yashid Khaled Kuzorski.

De mortuis nihil nisi Latin

Well, there I was, all set with something to say about Yasser Arafat at last, and then he ups and dies on me, and *de mortuis*, as they say, *nihil nisi bonum*. Only they don't say, of course, because it's Latin.

I've got stacks of Latin floating around in my skull as a result of having it shouted into me by a man with vestigial malaria. Periodically the disease would cause him to collapse on the classroom floor in a sort of tropical sweat. It happened for the first time when we were in the third form and we duly panicked, sprinting to the staffroom for an adult and a mop. He tried pulling the same stunt three years later but by then we were sixteen and hairy and so super cool that we just sat around smoking cigarettes, playing poker and waiting for the bell, whereupon we left him on the floor for the next class to discover.

That story may be a tad exaggerated, but that's because it's a story and people have been exaggerating stories since they first put pen to papyrus. Take Homer, for example, as renowned a Latin poet as they come. He told monstrous porkies. Are we really supposed to believe that the Trojans went 'Ooh look, a wooden horse. How thoughtful of our eternal enemies the Greeks. Let's immediately haul it inside the city walls. Bound to come in useful some day.'? Precisely.

Meanwhile you can all put your pens down. No need after all to write the letter pointing out that Homer wrote in Greek. It was a trap, see, my own little Trojan horse.

Furthermore it was a trap with a purpose, conceived to illustrate the theme of today's little homily which I have just discovered and which isn't old beak-nosed Arafat after all. My theme is rather that the main use of learning is one-upmanship.

Take the Latin tag I rolled out in the first sentence. I'm perfectly capable of doing the same notion in English ('be nice to stiffs' does it neatly) but by whacking it out in a language as dead as Yasser I'm holding up a banner saying I'm frightfully educated. If you happen to be frightfully educated as well you're invited to join my smug little club.

But that doesn't mean we're friends. Because when a paragraph or two later I made an error about Homer, when, in short, I nodded (another classical allusion there. If you got it, give yourself a biscuit) what did you feel? Sympathy for poor benighted Joe? A fervent wish that everyone in this muddled world were as well educated as you? A lament for the decline of classical learning? Not a bit of it. If you're anything like me you felt the sort of bloodlust that my dingbat dog feels when he spots a possum in a bush. It's the chance to kill. Dingbat has developed the tactic of climbing the bank above the bush and then leaping onto the branches in order to dislodge the possum whereupon he kills it with relish and brings me the corpse, which suggests that he may not be entirely dingbat after all. But the point is that it's his equivalent of writing to the editor but much more fun. In other words, you and I and dingbat are all out there for one reason, which is to win. And good on us all, say I.

The Catholic church spotted the daunting show-off value of Latin from the beginning. By continuing to intone *in nomine* this and *in spiritu* that they kept the educationally deprived peasants in awe-struck tithe-paying subjection for the best part of 2000 years.

It's not just Latin of course. Consider quiz nights in pubs. I love them. They're just about the only reward I get for suffering through seven years of high school accruing nuggets like the date of Shakey's birth (1564) and his inside leg measurement in millimetres (ditto). All the history, geography, physics, algebra that I absorbed but never found a use for comes into its own at last. Up goes my hand and with it my self-esteem. Ooh, look at me, I know stuff.

In other words most so-called education is simply the tedious acquisition of a grab-bag of nuggets that we then spend the rest of our days longing for the chance to trot out.

But it's too late for old Yasser, I'm afraid, not that he isn't better off out of it, having spent the last few years living among rubble provided at enormous expense by Israel and with the only compensation being that he was an extremely long way from his dingbat wife.

And too late for my little commentary on him as well, not that it was really worth it anyway. All I had to say about him, apart from his having kept a hundred smug foreign correspondents in business for forty indistinguishable years, was that whenever I saw his face on the telly he reminded of an Australian netball coach. But *de mortuis nihil nisi bonum* so I'd better not say that.

Dead snapper

When I read that Henri Cartier-Bresson, the French photographer, was dead, I thought of Jill.

One summer in the early eighties I shared a second-floor flat with Jill in dismal north-east London. She worked for a publisher. I didn't work for anyone. I was back from abroad with money in my pocket and an electronic typewriter. I was going to write a novel.

Setting the typewriter on a table at the kitchen window was a mistake. These days my writing desk stands hard against a blank cream wall.

The window overlooked a line of backyards. Each was a few square metres surrounded by a tall brick wall. The yard to the left was a miniature jungle, crammed with a hundred shrubs and bushes in ornamental tubs, all so thickly flourishing that there was barely room for the old duck who owned the flat to squeeze between them with her little yellow watering can. Our backyard was bare concrete and a dustbin. The yard to the right was scattered with urban detritus – a tricycle on its side, a dead washing machine, a heap of nameless rubble, an engine.

The flat that gave onto that yard was rented by a Turkish family. I never saw the father. Mother was huge. Her children were sinuous and feral, like wild cats. They had shaved heads and sharp eyes. The games I watched them play were not war games. They were war. They shed blood. The youngest boy was especially vicious. He threw pieces of metal. He bit. He was about six. I watched him with fascination and wrote nothing.

Each evening Jill would ask me how my novel was going. I told her lies. One day she brought me a book. It was the one present she ever gave me. I gave her none but I did try to sleep with her. We'd been to the pub and talked suggestively. The memory is imprecise but, when we got back to the flat, somehow and dexterously she slid away from me and I expect I was relieved.

The book she gave me was called *After the war was over* and it consisted of black and white photographs. I have always preferred black and white to colour. It seems more faithful. These photos showed scenes from all over Europe in the years following the Second World War, snaps of celebration and misery, of ageing prostitutes in the ruins of Dresden, of children playing war games over the rubble that had been a church.

The photographs of one man stood out. When you turned a page you knew instantaneously whether the snap was one of his without having to read the attribution. That man was Henri Cartier-Bresson.

His photos captured not just the moment, but the meaning of the moment. A kiss by Cartier-Bresson was a single kiss between a returning soldier and a girl in a coat, but at the same time it was all kisses, it was the essence of kiss.

Whatever the talentless polo-neck-sweatered poseurs of the art world may say, photography can only ever be journalism, never art. Cartier-Bresson knew this. He called photography 'un truc mécanique' – a mechanical thing. In old age he threw away his camera and went back to brush and pencil.

Nevertheless his photojournalism was as good as it gets. It cut to the heart of things, gave the viewer a little thrill of seeing that yes, this is how it was, then at that moment. The ancient people in the photograph were people like me.

One afternoon when *After the war was over* lay open on the kitchen table beside the silent typewriter, the vicious Turkish child appeared alone in the derelict backyard. He carried a piece of what looked like bread and laid it with atypical care on the pile of rubble, then went back inside. I stared dreamily into the dim London afternoon, half-heartedly trying to think of words to write and writing nothing.

A pigeon as grey as the sky alighted on the tall brick wall. It checked for danger, fluttered down to the rubble, pecked a couple of times at the bread, swallowed it and took off. Twenty feet up it stopped in mid flight and fell through the air as if shot.

The Turkish boy emerged from the flat. He was whooping. In his hands was a short stout fishing rod with a fixed-spool reel. He'd hooked the pigeon.

He tortured it. He'd pay out line and let the pigeon gain altitude and speed, then yank on the rod and turn the bird from an arrowhead to tumbling chaos, all feathers and legs and panic.

I can see the image now as clearly as a Cartier-Bresson photograph, though I can't remember how it ended. With death, probably, but I expect I turned away.

I stayed with Jill the whole summer then went abroad again. My novel never happened. The typewriter's in a landfill somewhere. Cartier-Bresson is as dead as the pigeon. The Turkish child is probably in prison. And as for Jill, I haven't seen her for twenty years but I do know she no longer works for a publisher, or at least not directly. She's become a novelist.

O fish, which art in tank

I've found the cure for everything. Corrupt Dutch royalty, fat sweaty men in suits saying 'leverage', obsessive interest in the All Blacks or Tuscany, ennui, sex, I've banished the lot, knocked their little blips off the radar of my life and discovered peace. I've bought some fish. I should have done it years ago.

I got three of them second-hand, or pre-loved as the zeitgeist prefers us to say. They came in a bucket. The bucket was yellow, the fish, respectively, gold, silver and bronze. I've got a complete set of Olympic medals swimming around next to me right now and whether or not they were pre-loved they will certainly be post-loved. They will be pampered and cosseted. I have no idea what the difference is between pampered and cosseted but I bunged in both verbs just to reassure the fish that they've made it to heaven and that they will stay here till the day that they flutter a final fin. I'm nice to my animals, you see.

I've installed their tank, their world, on the breakfast bar that stands between my work desk and the kitchen. The breakfast bar has never once supported my breakfast, of course, things being used for their official purpose only in advertisements, but for a decade or so this breakfast bar has supported the cat's breakfast in the form of a bowl of biscuits. It has also supported the cat's lunch and dinner in the form of the same bowl of biscuits. What the cat will do when it discovers that its biscuits have been supplanted by a fish tank, I don't know.

I'm rather hoping that it will leap onto the said breakfast bar with the casualness of habit, collide with the tank and recoil onto my desk in stunned puzzlement. At the same time I am hoping that the cat won't conclude that I've changed its diet of inert biscuits for something a bit more challenging. On balance I expect the cat to stare at the fish in the manner of a child staring at a cake-shop window, or perhaps, to use a simile more in tune with the zeitgeist, in the manner of a child staring at a 37-inch plasma screen on which twelve-barrel Arnie is dishing out all twelve barrels to an assortment of gooks and low-lifes and taking time between rounds to drool over his own biceps in a rapture of narcissism before becoming governor of a state the size of Europe.

But whether or not the cat takes to staring, I already have. This is my first morning of fish, and I have spent most of it with my lower lip collecting saliva. Fish are made for staring. They don't do much. They've got a couple of holes in them. There's a mouth that can be extended like a small zoom lens and an anus that can't. Add a gill or two and a couple of gormless eyes and that's it, fish. Done and dusted. All over. Simplicity in scales. But oh, what a difference to me.

I can metaphorically chuck anything into the tank and cool off. If I read about Melville bloody Gibson making 500 tetrazillion dollars from some film about the crucifixion and pledging half of it to the Catholic church, and I find myself coming out in boils around the kidneys, I now just turn to the fish. 'What do you reckon, fish?' I say and they swim to and fro, faces in neutral. I can toss them anything at all. *Woman's Weekly* with its yummy Xmas recipes and exclusive pictures of some talentless Los Angelic bimbette frolicking on the beach with a swarthy toy boy, bank profits, bank décor, banks, dog laws, the MP for Rotorua, undersized meals on oversized plates, wine buffs, clairvoyants, car enthusiasts, into the tank they all tumble and the fish swim to and fro, not caring. And nor do I any more. Ha. Henceforth I'm going to be calm as Buddha, calm as a fish. Nothing will rile me. Advertising pimps, technology freaks, skateboarders with kneepads, peacemongers, warmongers, Super 12 souvenir lift-out sections, I shall consider them all with the lofty gormlessness of fish.

I'm going to change the calendar. History will be divided in two. Everything up until now and the advent of fish, will be consigned to a period known as BF, Before Fish, a period of bitterness and angst and frustration and perpetually boiling rage. But everything subsequent, everything from this moment forth, will belong to a new era, the AP era, Anno Piscis, the time of gormless calm. I shall be as emotionally volatile as putty. The even tenor of my dummkopf days and mood will be interrupted only by daily services of worship during which I shall toss sacramental offerings into the tank while intoning 'O fish, which art in tank,' in a voice as flat as a wet Sunday. It will be lovely.

It should last at least a week.

Good and gloomy

I'm a Larkin bore. Larkin's like herpes. Once you've got him, you've got him. You may pretend you haven't and you may even sometimes convince yourself, but then into your skull comes a vague thought, no more than a notion, and at the same time up pops Larx with a phrase that pins that notion down in words as precise and simple and memorable as crystal. And those words are always gloomy. Deliciously gloomy. 'Life is first boredom then fear,' wrote Larx. 'However you use it, it goes.'

'My wife and I have asked a crowd of craps,' wrote Larx, 'to come and waste their time and ours. Perhaps you'd care to join us?'

I evangelise for Larx. I bombard potential converts. Last Saturday over dinner I bombarded a cricketer and a young woman who works in television. I belaboured them with Larx. I socked them round the head with quotation. I crammed words down their throats. Whether they enjoyed it or not I don't know and I don't care. I enjoyed it and that's what matters.

But I was drunk and I got most of quotations slightly wrong. I could sense their wrongness but beer made me powerless to right them. The next day when I should have been working I reread the whole of Larx in order to fix the words more firmly for the next time

I went preaching, fix them so firmly that even a dozen Heineken couldn't slur them out of their immutable order.

The whole of Larx is not a lot. In his forty or so years of writing he published only a hundred or so poems. He wrote plenty of others and people published them after his death in order to cash in and I duly bought them and they're on the shelf beside me as I write, but Larx did well not to publish them. They're not as good as the hundred and the hundred are enough. The hundred are all. The hundred are his children. His children will not die.

My evangelism does Larx no good. It brings him no joy and it brings him no dosh. He's dead. He died in 1986 when I was teaching. I read his obituary in the paper when my class was writing essays. I told the children to stop writing, then I told them Larx was dead.

'And saying so to some,' wrote Larx, 'means nothing. Others it leaves nothing to be said.'

Larx left nothing to be said. And I miss him. I want more of him. I need him to pin down my gearstick.

My car's an automatic so the gearstick isn't a gearstick. All I ever do with it is to shift it from P to D, and then I go. The business of driving doesn't interest me and I distrust people that it does interest.

There are five other zones on the gearshift. I never use the imaginatively named 1 and 2 and 3 because if I'd wanted gears I'd have bought gears. There's also N, whose purpose I have never understood. But then there's R. R is a siren. R sings to me. R tempts me.

I'll be driving through the tunnel to Lyttelton all blameless and merry, and because there's nothing to see in a tunnel but walls and lights and bright ceramic tiles, I'll let my gaze go idling round the car and it'll alight on R. And when it does I'll feel an urge. An instantaneous reflex urge. An urge to grasp the gearstick when I'm doing a sober and blameless 60 kilometres per hour, and to depress the little knob on the side. I want to engage R. I want to. I want to. I want to. Almost. It's like the semi-urge I feel on cliff-tops. The urge to dive.

In one way I know why. I want to hear the sudden clunk of the engine, the momentary unthinkability of it. Momentary, I presume, because in half the time it takes to say 'perhaps that wasn't wise' the metal would sheer and the gearbox shatter and the car explode. Or so I imagine. And there's a sliver of me that wants to taste that, to see that, to be in that.

And then there's the black urge, the urge to destroy, the urge so brilliantly conjured by Graham Greene in *The Destructors*, in which a teenage boy conceives and executes a plan to demolish an antique house. The only reason the boy can find to explain his action is that the house is beautiful.

But beneath all that there's something else, some Freudian stream that underruns my consciousness. It's the sort of thing that only Larkin could enshrine in words, words that go thudding to the hub of things like three straight darts into the triple twenty. He will not do it now.

But then again perhaps he has. Perhaps, as always, things are simpler than I thought. It takes a Larx to show me that. 'Beneath it all,' he wrote, 'desire for oblivion runs.'

Isn't he good? Isn't he gloomy? He makes me happy.

I, speechwriter

I, principal speech-writer to the President of the United States of America, do solemnly swear to write a doozy of a speech for President Bush's – and gee, yeah, I'm as astonished as you are – second inauguration.

When coaching the president in the delivery of this speech, I do solemnly swear to try to stop him grinning like a schoolboy at being re-elected, though I am not confident of success. I shall also encourage him to clench his eyebrows during the serious bits of the speech and to stress the important words.

The most important word for him to stress is liberty (*applause*), which I do solemnly swear to use more than thirty times during the speech, partly because it always spurs applause (*applause*) but mainly because everyone approves of it without being able to define it. If I tire of the word liberty (*applause*) I shall substitute the synonym freedom (*applause*), though I shall not use the word synonym because of potential presidential pronunciation problems. Nor for the same reason shall I use the phrase 'potential presidential pronunciation problems'.

I shall exploit standard rhetorical devices such as the triple construction, the aim of which is not to create a reasoned argument, nor yet to pile evidence on evidence, but simply to sound climactic. A quality that the periodic sentence, of which I shall also make use, reserving as it does its principal word or phrase, most commonly the verb, right to the end of the sentence, sometimes at the risk of mangling the syntax and baffling the audience (*bafflement*), shares.

I further pledge to coin illogical extended metaphors, such as 'the fire that America has lit in the minds of men'. Of this fire I shall say that 'it warms those who feel its power; it burns those who fight its progress; and one day this untamed fire of freedom will reach the darkest corners of our world'. But what this selective fire will do when it reaches those darkest corners, I shall not say. I hope it doesn't burn them down as fires tend to do.

In the course of the speech I shall make great use of the abstract noun courage because it is sometimes induces applause (*silence*). But not always. Nevertheless courage combines with freedom (*applause*) to echo 'the land of the free and the home of the brave' and thus arouse patriotic fervour. Patriotic fervour achieves the first aim of an inaugural speech, which is to numb the power of reason.

The same is true of God (*reverential awe*). Therefore I do also solemnly swear to cram the speech with references to God (*reverential awe*). Not only will they induce a feeling of reverential awe but they will also align the president with the war leaders of history, all of whom from Julius Caesar to Osama bin Laden (*opposite of reverential awe*) have used references to God (*reverential awe*) or gods (*puzzlement*) to encourage their troops.

By these means I shall rewrite the truth of the conflict in Iraq. Rather than portraying it as a self-interested act of invasion, my words will make it seem a selfless act of liberation. And I do solemnly swear not to mention the lies about terrorist links and weapons of mass destruction that the president used to justify the self-interested act of invasion. Those lies are now history and I mean to ignore history.

Except, of course, when history is useful, for I intend to quote from the very historical Abraham Lincoln. This quotation will make the president look learned, will link him with an older and wiser president, and will provide me with another chance for a triple construction. It will also allow me to use the word freedom (*applause*) again.

According to old Abe, 'Those who deny freedom to others deserve it not for themselves, and, under the rule of a just god, cannot long retain it.'

But I shall not pursue these words to their logical conclusion because I do solemnly swear it would screw up the speech. For rather a lot of freedom-denying tyrants – Kim Il Jong, Mao Zedong, Joseph Stalin, Saddam Hussein (*opposite of applause*) and many another – have retained power for rather a long time. Indeed the first three on my list all managed to die in office. The only reasonable conclusion to draw is that there is no just God (*reverential shock*). At the same time it appears that the current president has adopted for himself the role of that just God.

Playing God is not a good look for a devout president so I do solemnly swear to leave the Abe-quote dangling. An inaugural speech does not exist to reach logical conclusions. It exists to appeal to the 90 per cent of Americans who believe in God. With any luck it will also blur the distinction between that God, the President of the United States, and American self-interest (*applause*).

After the speech I do solemnly swear to sink a lot of cocktails at each of the nine inauguration balls. And the reference to balls reminds me that it is time for the standard peroration. May God bless you and may he watch over the United States of America a bit more carefully than he did on the 11th of September 2001 despite constant reminders from every inaugural speech since 1776 that this was his number one priority (*thunderous and sustained applause*).

A box of revenge

Fool that I am, I did Mike a favour. One should never do favours because the recipient feels obliged to retaliate. Mike's retaliation came in a box. The box was the width of a pair of stretched arms. He had to turn it on its side to get it through the door of my house. The dogs barked at it.

'For you,' he said, 'a present.'

I opened the box. It contained a lot of squeaky polystyrene and a grey gadget dressed in cellophane.

'It's a printer,' he said, 'and a photocopier and a scanner and a fax machine, all in one.'

There are moments in life when you speak straight from the heart, when the words come with a gush of unstoppable honesty. This was not one of those times.

'Oh, thank you,' I said.

'It's compatible with your computer,' he said. 'I checked. You just plug it in and Bob's your uncle.'

Hitler had a similar manner of speech. 'You just march on Moscow,' he told his military command, 'and take it. Easy peasy.'

Having received his due of gratitude, Mike left, feeling, I suspect, much as the Greeks must have felt when they sailed away from Troy leaving behind them only a wooden horse.

This electronic horse came with an instruction manual. I didn't read it. I knew that its words would bounce off my mind, leaving no residue of meaning. I folded the flaps of the box back over and let the thing be. It would serve nicely as a coffee table.

I depend on my computer. It is a hugely convenient typewriter and post office in one. But like so many things that I use in the technological age, like my car and my telephone and my washing machine, I haven't the least idea how it works. And if it stops working I feel suddenly like a man with erectile dysfunction, if, that is, a man with erectile dysfunction finds the back of his head incandescent with frustration, rings a help line, can't understand the help, beats the desk and bursts into tears, which I doubt that he does.

Computers are like your health. When they go well, you take them for granted. But when they go wrong, they swell to block the sun. And just as with my health, I do nothing to maintain my computer when it is not going wrong. I don't install virus protection or dust it. Great mats of dust build up behind it and under it and on it and I am wary of touching them for fear that they have become integral to the machine's functioning. I fall back, in other words, on that old staple of the ignorant and timorous human being, superstition.

Then one evening last week Dave came round. Dave's a geek. He works with computers, speaks their language, knows no fear of them. He cleared the cups and the ashtray from my coffee table and opened its flaps and said, 'Well, what have we here?'

I told him what we had here. We had a multi-purpose machine that like all multi-purpose machines would perform none of its purposes satisfactorily. 'This,' I said, 'is an electronic Swiss army knife. And just as on a Swiss army knife there's a pair of scissors that's too small to accommodate an adult thumb, a saw that wouldn't saw its way through fishing line and a can opener that doesn't, so here there's a combined printer, scanner, fax machine, copier and, for all I know, a bleeding mortgage broker that is going to stay in its box because otherwise it will give me a bout of headaches so severe that my brain will melt and drip simultaneously from ear and nostril.'

'You mean you don't know how to set it up,' said Dave, and before you could say clouds of dust that would be a marvel in the Kalahari, he was pulling wires off the back of my computer. 'This thing's a fossil,' he said after a while and between coughs. 'You're going to have to update the OS.'

'Wrong on both counts,' I said. 'For one thing, the computer is only six years old, thank you, and for another thing, it will be you, Dave, who is going to update the OS, whatever that may be, otherwise the OS will remain emphatically unupdated and the electronic Swiss army knife will take the first plane back to Switzerland.'

Dave loves it when I talk dirty. Into the Internet he dived in search of the download that would bump my fossilised machine out of the twentieth century and into the excitingly different twenty-first. To my surprise but not his he didn't find it. In the world of information technology 1998 is ancient history, like the story of the Trojan War.

You've guessed the ending. I bought a new computer, of course. Or rather Dave bought it and installed it and attached it to the Swiss army knife and in exchange I handed Dave a cheque for $1750, which, as I'm sure you'll agree, is one of the most effective bits of retaliation since the Trojan horse. Don't do anyone a favour.

DNAisy

Francis Crick has died. Fifty years ago Mr Crick solved the riddle of DNA. I'll admit that to me DNA remains a riddle but Mr Crick can hardly be blamed for that.

His discovery made all manner of things possible. He himself lived long enough to witness the birth of Dolly the cloned sheep, an event that couldn't have happened without his research. He also, as it turned out, lived long enough to witness the premature death of Dolly the cloned sheep, but he can hardly be blamed for that, either.

According to a learned article that I read this morning and of which I understood several entire sentences, we share 99 per cent of our DNA with chimpanzees. This nugget of truth is yet another one in the eye for theology. For if, as the theologians have insisted for a couple of thousand years, God made man in his own image, those same theologians are now going to have to acknowledge that the chimp is a pretty faithful self-portrait of the creator as well. Of course the theologians are going to acknowledge no such thing. They've been weaselling their way around all sorts of inconvenient facts for a long time now. They weaselled round Copernicus. They weaselled round Darwin.

In order to weasel round the truth of DNA the whiskered

theologians will just shake a crabby finger, say 'ah but', and focus attention on the 1 per cent of DNA that we don't happen to share with our tree-swinging relatives. That 1 per cent, they'll say, is the divine spark. That 1 per cent makes all the difference. They're wrong about the divine spark, but they're right about the difference.

That 1 per cent must contain the blueprint for all the things that we do but chimps don't, everything from motor racing, power point presentations, celebrity chefs, *NZ Idol*, pornography, computer games, corporate English, All Black advertising, Ken and Barbie, rhythmic gymnastics, bank fees and dehumidifiers to the wholesale slaughter of daisies. It's a busy bit of DNA.

I mention daisies only because the author of the learned article also mentioned them. He noted in passing that we human beings, in addition to being virtual chimps, also happen to share more than 30 per cent of our DNA with daisies. In other words, up to about thigh level, you and I are plants.

The name daisy derives originally from 'day's eye' because daisies have the endearing habit of closing their petals at night like eyelashes and opening them again in the morning. Perhaps for this reason, the daisy has long been a symbol of humility and innocence.

The reward for this humility and innocence has been persecution. Despite being non-venomous, passive and pretty, daisies are vilified by the suburban gardener for daring to disrupt the uniformity of his lawns. To wage his campaign against them the gardener has a potting shed that resembles a storage room at the Pentagon. It's crammed to the roof beam with weaponry, some of it straightforward hardware like dibbers and trowels, but much of it chemical. What the gardener is engaged in is a holy war, a jihad.

For gardening is a religious belief of which the principal dogma is that some plants are good and others evil. The good ones are called things like *Anagalypta tremens* and cost a lot at the garden centre. The bad ones are called weeds and cost nothing. I can't say it makes a lot of sense to me, but then sense is perhaps too much to expect when one recalls that gardeners, like the rest of us, share 99 per cent of their DNA with gibbering chimps.

But this DNA business stretches beyond both gardeners and theologians. It stretches indeed to that most fashionable of entities, the environment.

We are supposed to care for the environment. We don't. For a start we are all as judgemental as gardeners. As any DOC official will tell you it is easy to raise money to save the waddling kakapo, but less easy to raise money to save the giant worm-eating snail of Taranaki. In other words, we like only the fluffy bits. Our care is sentimental.

It is also selfish. No one, for example, gives a fig about Greenland. But then a shock item on the news tells us the place is melting and everyone starts giving figs by the barrowload. We're scared that Cathedral Square is suddenly going to disappear under 6 feet of water, at which point of course the cathedral will be crammed with theologians saying that this is God's vengeance for our sinfulness and expecting a celestial lifeboat to splash down at any moment in Worcester Street in order to rescue the righteous.

But the whole point is that there is no such thing as the environment as something external that we should care for. The daisies, the kakapo, the snails, the chimps and you and me share vast chunks of DNA. There is no gulf between us. We're it and it's us.

Of course this has always been perfectly obvious from the beginning. The very fact that we will all croak is evidence enough. But that has never convinced us of our kinship to everything around us. Copernicus couldn't manage it. Nor could Darwin. And Mr Crick, for all the irrefutability of his science, didn't manage it either. We insist on thinking we're special. The 1 per cent difference between us and chimps is invincible vanity.

Story story

Here's a little story. Please judge it.

A famous woman rang. It was mid-afternoon so I was asleep. Out of dreams of sweet chaos I stretched an arm to the receiver. 'Hello,' I said.

'Hello,' said the famous woman, 'this is…' and she said her famous name. 'Will you help me?'

'Golly,' I managed not to say and I sat up in bed and hauled a pillow into the small of my back and lit a cigarette the better to luxuriate in the joys of helping someone famous.

The woman is famous for being on television. She is less famous for judging short story competitions, but that was what she had found herself doing and she was finding it hard. 'Joe,' she said, 'how do you judge a short story competition?'

'Piece of cake,' I said and I paused to draw on my cigarette, smug in a sense of expertise. 'You give the prize,' I said, 'to the best story.'

'Ha ha,' said the famous woman, and I replied 'ha ha' though I didn't think I had said anything funny.

'But how do you pick the best story?' she said.

'Well,' I said, 'let's make one thing clear immediately. The best story is not necessarily the best story.' I paused to allow her time to absorb this little apophthegm and blew, as I have been able to do since the two months spent in bed at the age of seventeen with a broken leg, a perfect smoke-ring.

'I see,' she said in the manner of someone who didn't.

'A story,' I said, 'is an artificial thing. It does not occur naturally. A story is like a joke. A joke is too neat for life itself. And just as a joke depends entirely on the telling, so does a story. Therefore the best story is not the best story, but the best-told story. Because by being the best-told story, it becomes the best story.

'Life is random, you see, and stories aren't. They are drawn from life but they tie life into a neat parcel, the string knotted just so, the corners of paper folded and fixed square in the manner that seems to come naturally to women but not to men. And the knotting, the folding, if you follow me, is the telling. Stories clarify the endless whirl of the world. Stories run as they should, whereas life has a habit of tripping you up with unpredictability, especially when you think you've got it under control. Stories may offer an approximation of life itself, with apparently incoherent details, but within those details there is coherence, a theme of some sort, a meaning. And often it is something that we wish was so, that bad people, say, get what they deserve, or that the smug suffer. Stories offer meaning in a meaningless world. They provide what Robert Frost, I think, called "a momentary stay against confusion".'

'I'm confused,' she said.

'Precisely,' I said. 'We all are and that's why we need stories. They straighten things out. They clarify the complex. Good stories endure for just that reason and they are hard to create. That's why most of the stories you read will be bad stories that won't endure.'

'So what do I do?' she said.

I said to look for the story that convinced her, that sucked her in, that made her want to find out what happened, that engaged her emotionally.

And if by some lucky chance there were two or more that did this, to choose the one where she didn't notice how well it was written. 'Because the best prose,' I said, 'is invisible. It appears to be natural. It appears to let the story tell itself.' At which point I leaned back into the pillow, confident that I had indeed clarified the complex. I put my cigarette once again to my lips.

'So,' she said in summary, and I was impressed by her grasp, 'I shouldn't choose the best story, but rather the story that is best told. And the story that is best told is the one where I don't notice how well it's told.'

'You're onto it,' I was going to say, but I didn't say it. Instead, as I went to remove my cigarette I found that it had stuck to my sleep-dried lips. My fingers slid along the barrel and pinched the burning end. 'Aaaagh,' I squealed, as the glowing burning end fell and 'aagh' again as it landed on my thigh, and I dropped the phone and leapt from the bed and banged at the sheets and sucked my fingers and rubbed my thigh, and found the cigarette end and scrunched the sheet around it and ran naked to the bathroom and doused the sheet under the tap.

'Sorry,' I said to the phone when I came back. But the famous woman had gone.

On the road

First impressions matter, so we should pity the tourist who flies into Christchurch. He gets off the plane, rents a giant snail shell known as a campervan and heads south on State Highway One. He is keen to discover the scenic wonder that is the South Island of New Zealand. He gets Hornby.

A tourist who has crossed the world for an eye-feast is unlikely to hyperventilate at Hornby. I have no doubt that if the tourist stopped he would find the citizens of Hornby living rich emotional lives and being kind to ducklings, but the tourist has no intention of stopping. Indeed if he broke down and found himself threatened with spending the weekend in Hornby, I suspect that even if he were Mr Jolly from Jollyton in the country of Jollivia he would soon be reaching for the weedkiller.

After Hornby come several kilometres of more Hornby: a string of settlements that seem not to have settled, stretches of industrial scrubland, some gloom-drenched forestry and a terribly scenic prison. Then the long dwindle of Christchurch culminates in Rolleston. A sign announces that the city fathers have read Rolleston's horoscope and pronounced it good. 'Rolleston,' says the sign, 'town of the future.' To the extent that it isn't the town of the present they are bang right. The tourist continues down State Highway One.

The title State Highway One sounds arterial, magisterial, big. It isn't big. It's a bugger. Very occasionally it expands to four lanes. More frequently it manages three. But most of the time it's two. And it's festooned with road signs.

The speed limit sign says that the maximum speed is 100 kph. It isn't. The agreed maximum speed on SH1 is 107 kph, which is also, as it happens, the agreed minimum speed. All traffic on SH1 aspires to travel constantly at 107. Except for tourist traffic.

The tourist is driving an unfamiliar vehicle through unfamiliar territory. He pootles at 90. Behind him a swarm of vehicles gathers. The drivers of these vehicles, thwarted of their right to 107 kph, fizz like wasps in a jar. The tourist doesn't know this but the authorities do, so they have erected signs to calm the wasps. 'Passing lane 4km,' say the signs.

So, 3.95 kilometres later the wasp closest to the campervan backs off a few metres in order to accelerate into the passing lane before the wasp behind can beat him to it. An excellent trick here, and one that several tourists adopt, is to occupy the right-hand lane. The fizzing wasps become furious wasps.

If, however, the tourist keeps properly to the left the whole swarm will strive to pass him before the passing lane ends amusingly soon. The wasps then roar ahead to swarm and fizz behind another campervan. By the time they reach the next passing lane the first campervan has caught the wasps back up.

The tourist is looking for the 100 per cent pure New Zealand of the brochures with its mountains, lakes and orcs. What he gets on this stretch of State Highway One is a landscape as flat as English beer and as interesting as Paul Holmes. It's all shelter belts, irrigation pylons and inexpressive sheep. The repetitiveness of the landscape is likely to make him feel woozy. He then passes a road sign that asks him if he's feeling woozy. It features a design like a wavy whirlpool receding into a steering wheel. If he doesn't feel woozy he will when he looks at the sign.

Assuming that he keeps wooziness at bay the tourist will discover two things about this country that don't feature in the brochures. The first is that the authorities love telling us about road safety. The second is that they do it badly. 'You're a long time dead,' says a sign featuring a snap of a wet cemetery. 'So what's the hurry?' It's all frightfully daunting, a stark reminder of the brevity of existence, but at the same time it's irrational. The fact that you're a long time dead is precisely the reason to hurry. The tourist wants to get as much sightseeing done as possible before the reaper announces harvest festival. The tourist also wants to spend as few as possible of his remaining hours driving State Highway One.

Another sign shows a hammer and a nail. The hammer is labelled, 'car going at 60 kph'. The nail is labelled 'pedestrian'. Two conclusions can be drawn. One is that a car going at 60 kph bangs pedestrians into the ground but otherwise leaves them unharmed. The other is that signmakers get carried away with metaphor.

And puns. 'The quick are the dead,' says another sign. This juicy play on words is not as irrational as the other signs. It is merely a lie. The evidence that the quick are still breathing trails the tourist in the form of a swarm of wasps.

But if he is lucky the tourist reaches Ashburton intact, quick, unhammered and wooze-free. There a huge sign greets him with the local civic motto. 'Ashburton,' it bellows, 'whatever it takes.' I'm afraid I can't tell you what the motto means but I can tell you what it takes. It takes the biscuit for the most absurd civic motto.

Hi ho

Hi ho, hi ho (and I am bellowing that hi ho with exactly the same anticipatory exultation as in the dwarf song), I'm off to see a medium. Or, as I like to think of them, an average.

(Have you noticed, by the way, how the word average has changed its meaning? (Not that I care whether you've noticed or not. I've noticed and that's all that matters here.) Average no longer means what it means. If a cricket team has had an average season or a resort has had average weather, then you know that the team has come bottom of the league and the tourists have got wet. Average isn't middling any more. Average is bad. Because, in a hyperised world, we want super, we want extreme, we want more intensity, more excitement, more records broken, more adrenalin, more, bigger, better, whee whee, oooh oooh, hyperventilation, acceleration, g-force, beyond the limits, beyond the pale, superfast, superheated, supernatural, which brings us back to the medium.)

I wrote rude things about mediums in a newspaper column a while ago and this medium read my words (no, I am not going to ask why she reads a newspaper when her super-receptive ganglions are already bombarded by a mass of paranormal information to which we normal chaps and chappesses are not privy) and she thought oooh, what a silly and wrong and insulting thing for this nasty columnist to say, and, good on her, she picked up a pen and wrote me a letter (and no, I am not going to ask why she didn't just telepathise me, because the answer is obvious. She is perfectly capable of telepathising, of course, but I, with my untuned rice-pudding brain, am incapable of receiving the message. For I, to change the metaphor to something utterly contemporary and horrid, am a muggle, the reference being drawn from that epitome of twenty-first-century dummkopf culture, Harry Bloody Yawn Yawn Potter.). In the letter the medium insisted that I didn't know what I was talking about and that if I cared to meet her she would prove, yes prove, the truth of her trade. I would be converted. The blinkers of scepticism would tumble from my eyes and I would behold for the first time in all its glistening auroral beauty the thrilling horse paddock of the supernatural.

I wrote back.

'Dear Miss Medium,' (I wrote.) (Ooh what a lot of brackets I'm having today, reflecting, perhaps, the omni-directional fecundity of my giant throbbing brain.)

'Good. Thank you. Yes. Let's meet.

'Lotsalove (as you already knew)

Joe'

And so tomorrow she drives down from sunny Napier and I fly up from sunnier Lyttelton and we meet on the steps of Parliament at noon and I have no idea what she looks like but she will clearly sense by a thumb-twitch or two that I am I, although in case she's suffering from some sort of ethereal static I have promised to wear a jaunty Tyrolean hat (green, with feather). And not just to wear it. The hat is also a provisional packed lunch. For I have promised that if, as she has promised, she sends me back to Lyttelton convinced of the existence of spooky things and life after croaking and all the rest of the extraordinary range of the extraordinary, then I'll eat the hat.

(I shall also be taking, though not wearing, some cheese and pickle sandwiches.)

What will happen at our meeting? Well, self-evidently, she ought to know and I should be in the dark. But the truth, as it happens (ha ha), is the other way round. She hasn't got a clue how tomorrow will unfold. And I, the muggle, the rice-pudding brain, the unreceptive receptacle, Mr Dull-as-dirt, know exactly what will happen. Exactly.

We'll meet. We'll laugh. She'll make jesting reference to my hat and its imminent consumption, in response to which I shall be suave and charming – no novelty in any of that, of course. Then we shall go to some coffee joint and over a brace of flat whites she'll ask me questions. (She has, to be fair, already vouchsafed that she will ask me questions. What she hasn't told me is why. But I shall tell you. She will ask me questions because without my answers she will be as deeply in the dark as a worm in a compost heap.)

From my answers she will draw inferences about me and my family and my friends and my inside-leg measurement and my everything, and she will suggest those inferences to me, subtly, hoping for unconscious indications from me (a nod of the head, a smile, a widening or crinkling of the eyes) that she is on the right track. And I will be supposed to be astonished. It's an easy trick.

But what she doesn't know is that she will be on the wrong track. Utterly the wrong track. Because I will tell her fibs. And on the basis of those fibs she will get in touch with, say, a one-legged aunt of mine who never existed, and I will say, yes yes, that's Auntie Peg and thus I shall suck her in, utterly, just as she and her kind have been doing to the world for ever, and encouraged by my encouragement she will blunder ever deeper into the dark night of wrongness, and I shall remain the gleaming white knight of truth and honesty and rectitude and throbbing brackets. (I'm looking forward to it.)

SNAFU

Well, the end of summer nears and it's situation normal. The weather's cooling again, thank God, the Pope's close to croaking again, no thanks to God, Michael Jackson's on trial again, my dog's killing possums again, my mother's having a birthday again, chicken flu's on the rampage again and I think I've bought a house.

Oh, the fuss people make about houses. There's a slew of television programmes devoted to them – house-swapping, house-building, house-hunting, house-titivating programmes – all of them unspeakable. The only conclusion to draw is that the prosperous world is retreating ever deeper into Fortress Home, raising the drawbridge, lowering the portcullis and shrinking from the nasty world that the same television has told them is awash with paedophiles and chooks that kill. Better, safer, nicer, wiser to stay at home, double deadlock the door and turn the telly on.

But it's not just the telly. The real estate industry – anyone for oxymoron? – publishes glossy mags full of prose so purple you could paper a brothel with it and yet people seem to read those mags as eagerly as the Pope reads the Bible. They may not mumble the real-estate guff into a microphone in thirty-five languages, but they do appear to believe what it says. And if they believe that then they probably also believe the people who worry on our behalf in case we don't get round to doing enough worrying ourselves. According to the professional worriers not only is chicken flu about to send us all to the eternal coop, but buying or selling a house is difficult and causes stress. It isn't and it doesn't. In comparison with being a possum, or the Pope, it's a doddle. If you like a house and can afford it, you buy it. If you don't or can't, you don't.

It took ten minutes to buy my new house. I wonder how many bedrooms it's got. I spotted one with more than enough room for me and the dogs, and that'll do us. But ten minutes was five minutes longer than it took to buy the house I've lived in for the last ten years. When I first saw this place it was full of students and underpants. The students were lounging on sofas. The underpants were drying on the banisters. 'I'll take it,' I said. The students went away, the underpants went with them and everything's been fine ever since.

Same with selling. I've had more advice on selling this house than the Pope's had medical treatment. Clean the windows, nail a bit of trellis here, paint this, polish that, fix those, brew coffee, bake bread, don't smoke, burn vanilla pods to mask the smoke, shoot the dogs, hire an agent, hope like hell, take Prozac. I did all of these except the last twelve. In other words I organised for someone to clean the windows.

The first person through the place bought it. Half an hour later the window cleaner turned up. I should have sent him away but I didn't because he'd lugged his ladder all the way from town. Then he charged me extra because he said the windows hadn't been cleaned for five years. I didn't argue, but he was wrong. It was ten years.

But I have to admit the effect is nice. Lyttelton looks sparkling and I can now spot moribund chooks and passing paedophiles with 20/20 clarity. But clean windows haven't solved the annual problem of my mother's birthday.

Like the Pope, my mother's eighty-something. Physiologically God's been kinder to her than he's been to the Pope, presumably because she hasn't pestered him in thirty-five languages, but I still don't know what to get her for her birthday. If you really want something – walk-in wardrobes, matching ensuite bidet and spa bath, the papacy – by the time you're eighty you've either got it or else realised that you didn't really want it.

What's more you've also realised that you don't want most of the things you've got. So old age becomes a business of shedding stuff rather than acquiring stuff, of reverting to childhood when a toothbrush was one possession too many, or to doghood in which the sole possession is a collar, and dogs want collars about as much as I want to be the next Pope. Which is all just dandy for my mother of course, but it doesn't help a distant son when he needs to buy a little birthday something to say the sort of stuff that he ought to say but doesn't get round to saying because, well, he's a son.

I've spent twenty times as long present-hunting as I did house-hunting and I've come up with as much good stuff as you'll get at Michael Jackson's trial. But now I've had an idea. I think I'm going to organise a birthday visit from the window cleaner. My mother's a bit past ladder-lugging. And after the man has gone she'll be able to look out and observe with renewed clarity that the world is every bit as bizarre as it was when she first caught sight of it eight decades ago. In other words, situation normal.

Let's boulder

When you're frolicking on the hills with a song on your lips and a pair of dogs, and you see a bloke lugging something big up a track, it's only natural to stop and say hello and to ask what the thing is. I stopped and I said hello but I didn't do much asking because the thing was obviously an easel in a case. The man was planning to climb to a scenic niche and then daub something pretty for the tourists or for his own satisfaction or for both. Nevertheless etiquette required me, I thought, to point at the easel case and say 'What's that?', so that the bloke could have the pleasure of telling me with calculated modesty that he was, oh dear, an artist and he was going up the hill to do sensitive creative things and please would I feel both envy and admiration.

And then perhaps I might offer to carry his brushes or smock and together we would climb to a panoramic eminence where I would stand behind him with feigned reverence and genuine curiosity while he laid the first tentative smears of acrylic. And because I had time on my hands, and because I looked forward to privately not thinking much of his painting, and because the dogs would relish another hour sniffing through the undergrowth for something to kill, I pointed at the easel case and said, 'What's that?'

'A bouldering mat.'

'Oh,' I said. Then because that seemed a little unforthcoming, I added, 'What's it for?'

'Bouldering.'

'Oh,' I said. 'Can I watch?' and off we went up the hill together, him carrying his mat and me carrying nothing but enough curiosity to kill a medium-sized cattery.

We climbed to the disused quarry. A hundred years ago they blasted and hacked great cubes of sharp volcanic stuff out of there, but now a grass as fine and soft as maidenhair has carpeted the quarry floor, and scrubby bush has masked the scattering of rocks. The port is out of sight and earshot and the place is windless. It's like a tank of vegetative silence. I've often sat there long and long and thought the place was mine alone. But clearly the boulderers had found it too.

The man led me through the scrub and then he stopped at the quarry wall and laid his mat at the foot of a rock the size of a garage door. Its face was as smooth as a girl's. He shed his jacket, then round his waist he slung a pouch like a Renaissance purse. I asked what it was for.

'Weightlifter's chalk,' he said. He took off his tramping boots and socks and replaced them with a pair of blunt-nosed ballet shoes made from rubber. 'The same stuff they make Formula One tyres out of,' he said.

Bouldering seemed to need a lot of stuff. I don't like stuff. I would, for example, be more likely to go skiing if it didn't require so much stuff: boots, skis, poles, goggles, hat, gloves, ski-pass, four-wheel drive, artificial sun tan, and all for a bit of sliding. These days I am content with a snowless hill and two dogs.

The boulderer sat on his bouldering mat at the base of the rock. He chalked his hands and gripped two tiny ripples in the rock. He nestled one rubber toe into a crevice as deep as a wrinkle on a Labrador's forehead, wedged the other against a protrusion the size of a nipple, and hauled himself up. Though a mere foot or two off the ground he was clinging to the vertical face like a spider on a bedroom wall. He went on to climb the smoothness with deft, deliberate skill, wriggling each toe and finger separately into its niche before shifting his weight onto it.

'It's not about climbing as such,' he said as he climbed. 'It's about setting challenges and overcoming them. It's about technique. It's huge.'

A minute later he was standing on the summit of the boulder. If I'd stretched I could have touched his toes. The boulder's face was dusted with the chalky traces of its conqueror's fingers.

I asked him if he ever fell. 'Sometimes,' he said as he climbed back down. 'That's what the mat's for. But you don't get injured bouldering. Not like mountaineering. Mountaineering's how I broke my back.'

'Oh,' I said, and then 'I see', and thanked him and left. But I wasn't sure that I did see. And as I called the dogs from their forest of smells and went mundanely down the hill on foot, a host of notions flooded through my head. Notions of pointlessness and purpose. Notions of the primitive need to conquer and how at heart we hate the barren sterile safety of the urban twenty-first century and have to engineer synthetic thrills. But then I remembered a night a quarter of a century ago when I climbed to the roof of a parish church and stood in moonlight whooping to the dark and silent village down below. But then again, at the time I thought I was in love.

Only the hard stuff

Some of my regular readers, and possibly both of them, will want to know whether I ate my hat. It was, they may recall, a jaunty hat of Tyrolean design complete with feather and I was taking it to meet a lady medium (which sounds like a bra but isn't). And if, as the lady medium promised, she proved the truth of mediumship, then I would eat the hat.

But first I feel the need for a sentence like an anaconda sated with subordinate clauses in order to capture an image that is fresh and remarkable in my mind but that will soon fade as so many fresh and remarkable images have faded because of the wilting middle-aged memory stick, an image that I met this morning on the hills where the dogs and I had gone for a dawn frolic before the heat of the summer day came stomping in from the nor-west to drive the three of us under the house panting, and there, right there at the top of the Port Hills where the Bridle Path meets the Summit Road at a spot of designated prettiness, a place at which you will meet no one in winter but an occasional earnest tramper in the sort of shorts that suggest sexual deviance, but where in summer the tourists often stop their rental vans and climb down from the passenger cabin in order to absorb the spectacle of sea and mountains and are bored within minutes unless another rental van stops and supplies them with a fellow tourist with whom to agree on how spectacular the spectacle is and how very much they are enjoying being entranced by it, there, right there, at the very apex of the land, was a car. It was a Mitsubishi.

Nothing remarkable about that, of course, just as there is nothing remarkable about someone claiming to be a medium, spurious spirituality being almost as old as the basalt of the Port Hills. But this car was different. It was dead. Seriously dead. As dead as the disembodied characters that mediums would like to convince us they chat with.

It was clear what had happened to the car. The thing had been stolen during the night from some summer-warm suburban street where all the citizens were sleeping under thin sheets having spent the evening with the television on. The thieves could only have been young men, youths, boys resisting the pull of the suburban street and the zippered jacket and the fawn slacks and the thin sheets and the early bed and the million evenings of television. They stole the car then drove it for joy, ahead of the nor-west wind, as drunk as skunks, screeching the corners of the Summit Road, and then at the highest point, they stopped the car and torched it. There at the designated beauty spot where the nor-west makes the tussock stream to lee, they set fire to the car in the middle of the night. It would have burned like a beacon. If I hadn't been sweating in bed beneath a single thin sheet I would have been able to see it from my deck, screaming flames against the sky's ink.

Are you really still waiting for news of the medium? Why? Do you imagine for one minute that Mademoiselle Clairvoyante may have been genuine? Is there still, in defiance of all reason, all evidence, all transparent fact, a part of you that does not find the fierce and fascinating surface of the earth enough and that yearns for something supernatural, something enduring and beyond and, oh my God, spiritual, something suggesting that this life is merely a sandwich stop on the long road to destiny and fulfilment? Really? Is there?

Well, you should have seen the car. It told the story.

It had been a plush car, a thing of gadgets and deep upholstery that held its passengers like a plump warm lover. A cocoon of comfort, a lounge suite on wheels. But not any more. The fire had licked all that away, had vaporised the plump stuff, the yielding stuff, the softness. The windscreen had shattered with the heat and some of the glass had melted, dripping over the steering column like a Dali painting. Apart from the melted glass only the hard stuff was left, the honest bones of metal.

The headrest thing that is supposed to stop you getting whiplash was just an inverted metal spade, its corners square and hard and sharp. The seats were charred springs, the steering wheel a simple metal hoop, the doors just scorched and hollow panels packed with wires and levers. It was ghostly, gaunt and compelling, the skull beneath the flesh, consumption consumed. I stared at it as a tourist stares at a view or a medium a crystal ball.

It won't be there tomorrow. The authorities will take it away. We must needs be sheltered from its rawness. It will be buried in an unmarked grave.

And my Tyrolean hat, as you may perhaps have guessed, is intact, its feather still jaunty.

There you go

'Don't you think,' he said, 'that it's a poem?'

'A poem?'

'Yes, a three-word poem, apparently as dull as porridge, but deep within its three short words it generates a mass of boiling bubbles fraught with meaning, drifting up and through the thickness of the porridge till they reach the surface and expire with little gasps like soft and fragrant farts.'

'You what?' I said.

He didn't falter. Indeed I don't believe he heard me. His thoughts had flown a thousand miles away from me and from the lunch that lay before us on the wonky café table, the bacon, lettuce and tomato sandwiches, the cups of coffee, the water that the serving girl had brought although we hadn't ordered it.

'You see it everywhere,' he said, 'and that itself is irony. It is precise and local and yet simultaneously universal.'

'Just stop right there,' I said, a sandwich halting halfway through its journey to my mouth. 'I'm not the sharpest pencil in the box, so I'd be grateful if you'd slow right down and make it clear in words that someone literal like me can understand, precisely what it is that you're going on about.'

He froze. My words had hit the mark. A look traversed his face as on an astronaut who's staring at the limitless and thinking thoughts that grope towards the very underskirts of God when suddenly he gets a call from home to tell him that the plumbing's sprung a leak, the cat's gone missing and his son's got mumps. 'Okay,' he said, 'I will.'

'That's good,' I said, and set about my sandwich.

He laid his own aside. He wiped his mouth and chin, then blew his nose into the tablecloth and let it fall. I felt a little queasy.

'You are here,' he said.

'I am,' I said.

'No, no,' he said, 'you fail to understand. I'm talking of the words you see on maps of town or at the entrances to parks or zoos. The zoo or park or town is all laid out as if it had been sketched from up above where Big Boy lives, but in the bottom corner, by a small red dot that several million thumbs have touched and smeared and blurred, stand three small words. Those words are "You are here".'

He paused. I chewed. He seemed to want me to say something clever.

'Yes,' I said.

'You've got it,' he exclaimed, and leaping from his seat he reached across the tablecloth and gripped my skull and smacked a kiss on top of it, a big wet loving kiss that left a splash of spittle and a mass of little balls of sodden bread high up where I had once had hair but now have only skin. 'Precisely,' he exclaimed, 'I knew you'd understand.'

'I don't,' I said.

'Oh come on now,' he said, 'forget the modesty. You've grasped the meaning of it instantly. You understand that *you are here*.'

'I do?' I said, and wondered as I said it whether I could find some way of getting out of there at once. The man was nuts.

'It's so magnificently simple, don't you see?' he said. 'Just three short words but those three words are all-encompassing. "Beauty is truth, truth beauty," said Keats, "that is all ye know on earth, and all ye need to know", and fools have been repeating it since 1821. But Keats was wrong. If he'd just thought a bit he would have struck a line through all that guff and simply written "You are here". It says the lot.'

'You mean to say…'

'Of course I mean to say,' he said, his fervour causing flecks of scum to gather at the corners of his mouth. 'I always mean to say, but oh how rare it is for words to say precisely what we mean. Yet there, in "you are here", is everything, the existential essence, the cruel constraints of time and place, and yet the sense of infinite potential, the paradox we know as being alive.'

'And furthermore,' he added, and if I'd tried to stop him now it would have been like holding back a freight train with a rubber band, 'it is the only statement you will ever come across that is perpetually true. It is the whole of Shakespeare's canon in just three short words. It states the only thing we know for sure and summarises all there is to know. Three tiny simple words cooked up I don't know when or where by some forgotten functionary and yet it asks the great eternal question and demands the only answer any one of us can give.'

He paused and seemed immersed in thought.

'Yes?' I said.

'Exactly,' he said, 'yes.'

'I'm out of here,' I said.

'That's very neat,' he said, and smiled, 'but quite impossible.'

I left.

She told him good

She did him and she did him good. Real good. I wasn't there but he told me all about it, and I trust him. You would too. It's his handshake, or to be more precise his hands, or to be even more precise the skin of his hands. It's soft, the sort of soft that when you shake his hand you go ooh and want to hold on, to retain the softness for a while. I'm not talking limp. I try never to talk limp. No, his handshake is as firm as you could wish, but the skin, whoa, it's baby skin, flesh-of-a-peach skin, remarkable, wantable, nice. And it's sixty-something years old, this skin.

But soft skin and all, this woman did him. She did him good. Perhaps if she had touched the skin and gone ooh, things would have turned out differently but she didn't so she didn't and they didn't.

First she wrinkled her nose and turned to look at him, to register exactly what she expected to register, and then she turned away again, pointedly, noticeably, a turning away that implied unfinished business, implied, indeed, even at this early stage, that she would not rest until she'd done him. Done him good.

He noted her nose-wrinkle, her look, her turning away. He wondered whether it would lead to more, but he said nothing, did nothing. He's a gentle man, and a gentleman, a man of courtesy and consideration. He'll tell you if you ask him why his hands are so soft, though you do have to ask him because he is reluctant to speak of himself. And if he does, he takes care not to bore.

'Lanolin' is his answer. Lanolin made his hands soft. Not, of course, that he went each morning to a dressing table twinned with his wife's, a table set with mirrors and unguents and lotions and paints and brushes and powders and I don't know what else that the appalling cosmetic companies have been foisting on women for as long as vanity has been in the world and fear of rejection and fear of time passing. Oh no, he didn't apply the lanolin to his hands. He isn't what has been dubbed a metrosexual, a term that ought to mean the sort of men who masturbate on buses, but actually means those even more appalling men whose ambition is to present a lifestyle show on television and who wear their expensive printed shirt-tails outside the waistband of their trousers and who have succumbed to the cosmetic companies' understandable desire to double the size of their market by beckoning men into the fold of their expensive delusion, No, Mr Softhands is not a metrosexual. He's a retired wool-buyer.

The woman who did him didn't know that. She knew just two things about him. She knew that he was sitting a yard or two from where she had chosen to sit. And she knew, oh, golly did she know, that he was smoking a cigar.

It was a fat cigar and a costly one because Mr Softhands did well as a wool-buyer. He owed his success to those hands of his. Forty-something years he spent in the wool trade, buying and selling fleeces on the information that his fingertips sent upstairs, the honed nerve ends of those soft soft hands telling him all he needed to know about the fineness and the strength of the wool they were touching, the wool from which they were constantly absorbing the beneficence of lanolin. Those hands were the gentleman's unbuyable unsellable assets, his competitive advantage. But now he and his hands have retired and on a fine summer morning with nothing for him or them to do he gave them a cigar to hold.

The woman turned to him a second time. 'Do you mind?' she said, but it wasn't a question. It was a statement backed with all the delight of having a justified grievance. She knew that the times were on her side, whispering in her pierced ear that she was inviolable and pure, an Atkins-dieting gym-going saint, a favoured one, the future of the planet, the way things will be. And he was yesterday, a husk. Moreover he was a husk that was emphatically in the wrong, a husk that was violating her inviolability. 'Do you mind?' she repeated, her voice as arch as a bridge.

Mr Softhands looked back at her. Despite his hands he isn't weak of will. But he knew what gave her the strength to do-you-mind him with such venom. He's not so old that he can't see which way the zeitgeist geese are flying.

He wondered briefly whether it was worth pointing out that he had got there first and that the cigar had already been alight when she sat down not far away. He wondered furthermore whether it was worth pointing out to her that…but it was obviously futile.

'Good day to you,' he said – he was, as I have said, a gentleman – and he rose slowly to his feet and took himself and his hands and his impeccable manners and his offensive cigar away. And where did all this happen? At a café? An airport? At an outdoor theatrical performance? No. This encounter took place not far from Christchurch on a thinly populated beach.

Dear College of Cardinals

To: CollofCards@Vatican.com
CC: All World Leaders
Subject: Job Application
Dear College of Cardinals,
Forgive the email but I gather I've got to be quick. Besides, I don't trust the post. The only Italian postman I ever knew was not what one would call conscientious, being only too ready on a warm day to hear the call of the grappa and dump his sack in the Tiber.

Anyway, I'll come straight to the point. I want to be Pope.

I'm sure you're up to here with applications for the job, but before you toss this one into the furnace under St Peter's – and the heating system, by the way, is one of the first things I'd get fixed, by fiat if necessary (though not, for obvious reasons, by Fiat) – I'd just like to point out what makes my application different.

I haven't included a mug shot. That's because I'm flexible. I'm white, of course, but if, as the rumour goes, you're looking for a black bloke this time round, then I'm quite prepared to make with the Nugget. Nor will you catch me complaining that choosing a black bloke because he's black is every bit as racist as not choosing a black bloke because he's black. No, I'm happy to go along with whatever you say. I just want the job and will do what's necessary.

I'm not bothered about salary. So long as there's something dropping into a Vatican Bank Accumulator account every month, I'm not going to haggle about how many zeroes are dangling on the end of it. I realise too that there won't be any pension provision, this not being a job from which you retire, though if you want to throw in a termination clause on the grounds of senility, a gaga get-out as I believe it's known, then that's fine by me. In other words, you dictate the terms and I'll just sign on the dotted. Getting the picture now? I want this job.

Don't worry that I'm an unknown. Who'd heard of old John Paul when he was ministering to the vodka-sodden round the back of Warsaw Cathedral, eh? Precisely. As you and I know, fame comes with the job. And I want it. I like idolatry. Not that I'd call it idolatry, of course, that being fairly strictly verboten in your church (or rather, *our* church, if you see sense) but I was greatly struck by the recent funeral, queues visible from space, people coming down the steps towards the waxwork papa clamping a hankie to the eyes with one hand and toting a camera-phone above their heads with the other. That's good for business, my friends. It's the sort of stuff I intend to foster not only post-mortem, but pre. Performance popery will be my catch-cry. We're talking celebrity. John Paul set the ball rolling. I'll give it a bloody great shove. You'll love it. I'll have them signing up all over the globe. I'll cram the pews.

The theology I'll leave to you. Just tell me which bits of the Bible we're going to take literally and which bits we're going to deem metaphorical in order to avoid their nasty implications, and I'll do the rest. But could I suggest a pretty staunch unwavering style. Not too many u-turns on the basics. You know, birth control, abortion, creation, female clergy, homosexuality, all the old chestnuts. It's just that the main competition these days are those blokes in the desert, much given to fanaticism, and the only way to compete with fundamental stuff like that is to offer equally fundamental stuff. It gives the punters a life raft to cling to amid the shifting seas of tolerance and liberalism. Everyone pretends to want tolerance etc. but it requires work. What they really want is a set of rules, and then they can just get back to watching six thousand channels of scabrous trash from the great couch of indolence, secure in the knowledge that all the moral issues have been resolved once and for all by the representatives of him upstairs, in other words us.

Not having seen the books, I can't give you a detailed business plan, but I can tell you that I'll be shaking things up a bit. You lot have always been good at real estate, and that sale of indulgences stuff you used to do was a wheeze which might be worth another look, but otherwise, frankly, you're hopeless. I mean, how much did you get for the TV rights to the funeral? Exactly.

My model will be one of the Super 12 rugby franchises down this way, the Crusaders to be precise. (What a pity that title's been taken.) I'll exploit all available methods of marketing to build up a fan base: TV promos, collector cards, stirring music (that's something you've got a head start on) and so on. I want to see 'Don't cross the Papa' plastered across the back bumper of every clapped-out Volvo in Christendom.

What we need, you see, is unswerving loyalty to the cause, because you don't have to be Thomas Aquinas to see which way the global geese are flying. There's a showdown looming. East meets West. Islam meets Christianity. It'll be just like the glory days of a thousand or so years ago. And when it comes to a showdown, wishy-washy secularism just doesn't cut the mustard. What's needed is dogma plus a figurehead, someone the punters revere and believe in. And that, my clothy friends, should be me. Be bold.

I look forward to hearing from you.

In hope

Joe.

Mine's a double

You know how it is. You amble into a bar, exciting libidinous glances from one sex and envious ones from the other, all of which you ignore with the aplomb for which you are known but which none dare mention within your earshot. Odd thing, earshot. What about eyeshot, noseshot, tongueshot? Especially tongueshot. I'm going to adopt tongueshot. I shall define it as the maximum distance in a wind of less than 5 knots at which you can abuse an educational theorist and guarantee accurate transmission of the information from your jaws to his flappy little hair-tufted ears.

Anyway, within the crowded bar you shoulder aside the puritans, government inspectors and other droop-shouldered ghouls who are there merely to ensure that no smokers are having a good time, and with one flick of an aristocratic eyebrow you indicate to the fawning and awe-struck bartender that you are prepared to imbibe a foil-necked bottle of something chilled and he says – well, let's deal first with the things he doesn't say. He doesn't say, 'How has your day been so far?' because he is not a corporate lackey drilled in false courtesy. Nor does he say, 'And was there anything else with that, sir?' because he is not a corporate lackey drilled in transparent salesmanship. He says, 'Joe, your double's just come in.'

He's not talking horse-racing. He's not talking spirituous liquor. He's talking lookalike. He's talking doppelgänger. He's talking mirror image of your uniqueness. That face of yours, that physog, that sublimity that fronts you, that introduces you unfailingly to the world, as rugged as Rushmore and unique as a thumbprint, isn't. Someone else has got it.

Well, correct form at this point is to lay a brace of thumbs on the barman's trachea and squeeze. Grateful for the attention from your uniqueness he will offer no protest as he turns the colour of a ripe Victoria plum, whereupon you let go, plant a sloppy great kiss on any of his cheeks and tell him you just love his sense of humour. And that's that. Or at least it should be.

But it wasn't for me last night. The script to this point went as outlined but as I picked up my beer and headed for the great outdoors where the good people dwell, feeling that I had satisfactorily awed the kill-joys and underlined my reputation for casual violence, the barman spoke. I kid you not. He spoke. He said, would you believe it, no.

You can imagine my reaction. No is not a monosyllable to which I am accustomed. I swivelled.

'No what?' I said.

'No, look,' he said and he pointed. A stinging lecture on the grammatical and rational absurdity of 'no, look' sprang fully formed to my lips but though the barman was well within tongueshot, for some reason I did not deliver. Instead, and I cannot explain or condone this, I followed the line of his indicative finger. And I beheld, well, let us consider.

Most of us have a face. The odds are good that you've got one. How do you feel about it? In the silly years of adolescence you probably hated it. It was not the face you deserved. It was a bad face, too fat, too thin, too red, too white, too freckled, too drawn, too undrawn. But gradually as the years rumbled tank-like across the battlefield of time, your face changed. Chance battered it. Worry etched it.

Love lit it. Despair wrenched it. Your face spoke for you every time, whether you wanted it to or not. You tried to lie with it but it gave you away. And bit by bit it stopped being the face that wasn't right, the face that should have been other and that would have made all things well, and it became, well, your face, the only face possible. Not loved, perhaps, not cherished, but not hated either. It was a poor thing, but your own. A skin map of your past. Your unembellished CV. Your self.

At sixty, said Auden, everyone gets they face they deserve.

So imagine how I felt being told that, after forty-seven years of random batterings and chance emotions that had been mine and mine alone, my face, my front, my self, was not unique.

The barman was pointing at a man as middle-aged as I. Like me he was thinning upstairs in a dignified manner. Like me he was sipping a beer, the same brand, in fact, as I habitually buy. But there the similarity stopped. The face I was looking at was weak of chin and bland as a rusk. It was quite without character.

'Ho ho, barman,' I exclaimed, in much relief, 'ho ho. Ho ho. You think that's what I look like? Think again.'

'You could be twins,' said the barman, 'identical twins.'

'Ho ho,' I said again, 'you couldn't be more wrong', and I looked around the throng for confirmation.

'You could be twins,' said a twerp beside me.

'You could be twins,' said everybody.

I gawped. My supposed double was gawping too, staring at me and gawping.

'Do I look like you?' I asked.

'No way,' he said.

'Quite right,' I said, and bought the man who didn't look like me, a beer.

A land fit for tourists

When I read that cars were to be banned from Cathedral Square at night so that tourists could sleep soundly in their hotels, I knew at once who was behind the move. I went to see them.

In the quiet suburban street a woman was tending her scrap of front garden and an elderly man was walking a youthful dog. Did these people know what their street harboured? I doubted it.

The front yard of number 37 was a little less kempt than others but not enough to attract attention. Curtains were drawn across the ground-floor windows. I knocked.

'Joe?'

'Yes.'

The door opened just wide enough to let me in. Before my eyes could adjust to the gloom I was pushed against a wall and hands like butterflies frisked my legs and torso.

'A precaution, you understand.'

I understood. My years in down-and-dirty journalism have taught me something.

When the light came on I found myself in a bare kitchen. At the table sat a man whose face was hidden within a deep hood. I could just make out the ghosts of his eyes, flitting, nervous, intense. Before him on the table lay a pile of batteries, two digital alarm clocks and some sticks smelling faintly of almonds.

I went straight to the point. With people like this you don't mess around.

'The car ban in the Square,' I said. 'Your doing?'

'It's a start,' said the man in measured tones. 'But only a start. PETT's demands are extensive and we shall not rest until ...'

'PETT?'

'People for the Ethical Treatment of Tourists,' he said. 'We wanted a title that the public would remember. And believe me, they will soon remember it. Nothing's going to stand in our way.'

'Are you terrorists?'

I sensed the man stiffen. 'Was William Wilberforce a terrorist when he stood up against slavery? Was Mahatma Gandhi a terrorist when he sat down against colonial oppression? Every hero starts as an outlaw,' he said, deftly attaching a wire to an alarm clock as he spoke.

'But tourists aren't...'

'Tourists are people too, you know. Do you not realise that without tourists the economy of this country would collapse? Caring for the quality of their lives makes economic sense. But more, far more, than that, it makes moral sense. It's a moral imperative. Look what we subject tourists to. We herd them into buses like so many stock units and lug them off to see scenery. Have you ever considered how tedious scenery is? Day after day of mountains, glaciers, bush, river valleys, with nothing to do but take pictures. No variety, no stimulus, no challenge, just suffocating boredom. Then we cram them into identical hotels where the gift shops – or, would you believe, gift shoppes – offer paua shell coasters, manuka honey hand cream, commemorative pottery, stuffed kiwis and child-sized All Black shirts. Does nothing stir within you? Do you feel no sympathy at all, no urge to better these people's lives?'

I said nothing.

'We fly them into our major cities from all parts of the globe, but do we tart those cities up to entertain them? Do we fill the streets with significant experiences? We do not. We offer tourists the unvarnished sight of people going to work, rain falling and mothers grocery shopping, and then we expect them to lie awake at night listening to our boy racers hooning round the Square. It's archaic. It's intolerable. It's inhumane. Tourists don't come to see things as they are. They come to see them as they ought to be, and we're going to make sure they get them.

'Things are beginning to happen already. Near Rotorua there's an indoor farm, and also several cultural centres where indigenous people dress down and pretend to be primitive, and around Wellington it's possible to go on a Lord of the Rings location tour and stand on the exact spot where Gath slew Magdor, but these are still only tiny oases of excellence in a vast tourist desert. Where are our truly attractive attractions? Where is our Disneyland?'

'But aren't tourists free agents? Aren't they at liberty to come here or not?'

'Don't make me laugh. Are lambs at the works free agents? No, tourists are pushed from behind by the sheepdogs of wealth and boredom, and pulled from in front by the lure of brochures and fantasy. They deserve better. They deserve a world engineered to their gratification, and we at PETT aim to give it to them. We're going to change things and we don't care how we do it. You can tell your readers if you like.' He paused. Then from deep within the hood there came a mirthless ominous laugh. 'But it doesn't matter if you don't. They'll be hearing from us soon enough.'

It was after midnight when I left. Half an hour later I was standing in eerie, traffic-free silence at the heart of Cathedral Square. Around me I could sense the slow breathing of a thousand sleeping tourists, all undisturbed and unaware of what rough beast was slouching towards this country to be born.

Stay where you are

You don't want to read about sickness and I don't want to write about sickness, but I'm going to write about sickness because I'm sick. And when you're sick the only thing you can think about, unless you're terribly selfless and brave, which I'm not, is sickness.

I want to blame the sickness on something and my first thought was the bombs. Adrian gave me the bombs at London airport. They were blue. 'Take one with a double scotch,' he said, 'and you'll wake up in New Zealand.' I took two with a quadruple scotch and I woke up in Singapore. Or rather I was woken up in Singapore by a stewardess. I knew she was a stewardess because she was wearing the Singapore Airlines stewardess uniform that always reminds me for some reason of brothel curtains.

She woke me by pinching my leg just above the knee with a grip that they probably taught her in stewardess school. I don't remember what I was dreaming about but it didn't lead me to expect to be pinched on the leg. I lashed out at her. But stewardess school must have taught her about lashing out as well because she had withdrawn well beyond lashing range. 'Sorry,' I said, and she smiled a stewardess school smile.

The rest of the journey home was passed in a state of bombed grogginess, as if I was seeing everything through frosted glass. Even my dogs, who were kind enough to come and meet me at Christ-church, seemed furrier than usual.

But in the end I don't think I can blame my sickness on the bombs because it wasn't until forty-eight hours after I'd taken them that I fell sick. So I'm going to have to blame travel instead.

Don't travel. It brings nothing but grief. Travel is supposed to be a good. There are shops devoted to selling it. Those shops are bedecked with posters as predictable, corny and dishonest as an electoral speech in Tauranga. Beaches, sunshine, ruins and sex are the standard themes and they accord with reality about as well as I did with a brace of bombs inside me.

And yet the posters work. Paul Theroux was right to say that every traveller is at heart an optimist. Because however many times we discover that the beaches are boring, the sunshine elusive, the ruins ruins and the sex somewhere else, back we keep coming year on year for more of the same. We're hard wired to hope yet doomed to disappointment.

And nuts to the adventurers who say that travel builds character. According to a psychologist I was reading on the plane before the bombs dropped, character is more or less determined by the age of three and absolutely determined by the age of six. The remaining seventy odd years are spent coming to terms with what you can't change. But at least with character there's someone to blame. It all depends, it seems, on your parents. If they're nice to you early on, you turn out nice. If they aren't, you don't. If you're violent, craven, clingy, evasive, psychopathic or the MP for Tauranga, you can blame mum and dad. But you can't blame mum and dad for sickness. And neither can you blame your cat.

My cat welcomed me back by sulking in the garage for twenty-four hours. Then in the middle of the second night she slid through the cat door, jumped onto the bed, climbed over the dogs, curled twice around my head, purred for a bit then went to sleep. 'Nice to see you, cat,' I whispered. A short while later I felt cold. Then I began to shiver. And then I convulsed with a vigour that alarmed me and astonished the cat. At the same time something stirred in my guts with a rich twist of nausea.

I don't want to distress you with too many details, especially if you're reading over breakfast, but all I will say is that it would have been helpful if there had been a hand basin over which I could lean without getting up from the toilet. There wasn't. The ensuing half-hour in the dead and lonely middle of the night was less than fun.

When I was finally sufficiently drained to dare to leave my station I wrapped myself in a duvet and huddled in front of the log burner. I don't understand log burners.

Log burners are supposed to be more efficient that open fires because in an open fire a lot of the heat goes up the chimney. But with a log burner all the heat goes up the chimney. I'm sure some boffin would be willing to explain the science to me but I'm not interested. All I know is that I sat shivering in front of the log burner all night like a Dickensian orphan and that I'm still there now and that I'm still sick and that I can't find anyone to blame for it or anything else to think about. Sorry.

Pity Mr Shrimp

You've got to pity the freshwater shrimp. There are billions of them in New Zealand and they're all born male. Out they pop from Momma Shrimp fully formed and ready to head out and be blokes. Within minutes of being spawned they're drinking beer, shouting, leaving their clothes on the bedroom floor and frying all food.

The food they fry is detritus. I know so because I've just looked them up on the Internet and among the two billion bits of irrelevant pap that the computer dredged out I discovered the pleasing news that shrimp are detritivores. Detritivore is a word I've spent forty-seven years not coming across but now that I have come across detritivore I'm going to use detritivore as much as I possibly can in order to fix detritivore in the memory. Detritivore, you see, is precisely the word that I have hitherto lacked for describing the sort of vulture who pops round to your house and wonders whether perhaps you've got a little something in the fridge by way of a snack and then proceeds to eat his way through everything on the slotted white shelves, from heel ends of Stilton to the greenish sausages you were reserving as a treat for the dogs when they were especially good or at least not actively destructive.

But anyway, back to the young male shrimp chewing his way

along the stream bed or round the rocks of the aquarium with his transparent body, his ridiculously long antennae, his tiny digestive tract, his half a dozen spindly legs at the front, and his hairbrush of little wavy things slung beneath the belly that he flutters when he need to get a move on because he's late for the rugby. As he ripples on his way singing songs of male bonding and drinking rituals the little detritivore hoovers up other people's discards like one of those disquieting council vehicles with brushes on the front and a suction thing and a seemingly inexhaustible hunger for cigarette butts, leaves and condoms. Indeed whoever designed those vehicles may well have modelled them on the New Zealand freshwater shrimp of which I have several detritivorous specimens in the tank beside me all of which are equipped with, in addition to the stuff I've already mentioned, a set of tiny protruding thingies that sweep the detritus off the pebbles and into the undiscriminating oral orifice in much the same way as the council truck.

So all is well for the young male shrimp. He's got a bellyful of fried detritus, he's doing nicely at work by sucking up to the boss and he's thinking of bunging down a deposit on a low-slung Japanese car with a boom box and a supersize farting exhaust pipe, when one morning he wakes up to find that everything's changed. He's overwhelmed by strange feelings. He cares. Next thing he knows he's eyeing up his brothers in a manner that he finds frankly appalling, he's joined an aromatherapy class, he buys glossy magazines that he reads backwards, he fingers fabric, he enjoys shopping, he's developed a taste for slimming foods in monstrously fattening quantities, and he's learnt that the zodiac isn't actually an antique car but rather a coherent system of metaphysics deserving serious and detailed study.

Inevitably five minutes later he's horizontal on the shrimp analyst's couch bleating about the sudden, inexplicable and shocking way he's developed a taste for tofu. The analyst takes one look, strokes his belly hair in an apparently meditative manner, his own that is, rather than the upset shrimp's, and pronounces to the bewildered young thing that everything is perfectly normal, he's just suddenly turned female.

At which point the shrimp proves the analyst abnormally correct by bursting into tears.

Then, on the principle that if bad news is going to break it might as well come in a tsunami, the analyst casually adds, 'and you're pregnant'.

The shrimp, so astonished that she stops crying, fingers her belly and says that it feels like twins. The analyst has a quick fumble and announces in a flat tone of voice that at a rough guess it's quinquecentuplets.

'You what?' says the shrimp, reverting briefly to masculinity.

'There's about five hundred of the little bastards,' says the analyst. And that's that. The shrimp rolls off the couch and flutters down the road to buy bulk nappies. And read auras.

A woman read my aura uninvited last week and kindly sent me the results. What wasn't remarkable was that it was all tosh. 'You are a strong humanitarian,' said my aura. Ha. 'Compassion for others is evident.' Ha. 'There is a pureness of intent in your life direction.' Ha ha ha. But what was remarkable is that the darling managed to read my aura without meeting me. She just saw me on telly. Aura by pixels.

All of which I find perplexing, but not half as perplexing as I would find being a freshwater shrimp with its extravagant mid-life crisis. You've got to pity the little buggers.

Do you care?

Do you care? Oh good. Me too. I care like billy-o. After all, this is 2004, and we've transcended all that eighteenth-century nonsense about cultivating one's own garden and letting others cultivate theirs. The theme of the twenty-first century is caring. Caring, my darlings, is in.

I am a whirlpool of caring. I suck into my caring vortex everything that nice, caring Judy Bailey or even nicer and more caring John Campbell instruct me to care about. The Ukraine, high country tussock, chlamydia rates in Laos, lice in Laos, problem gamblers, melting icecaps, type two diabetes, type ten diabetes, I care about them all with such intensity that I sleep only eight hours a night.

And of course I'm not the only carer in this warm-hearted world, and neither are you. Caring is everywhere, praise be. Here's a story of caring.

There's a track on the Port Hills. My dogs frolic up it most days and I lumber after them, my bronchials squeaking like a nest of newborn mice. Every so often I stop on one of the several bluffs along the track to admire the view and to smoke the mice into silence.

The bluffs in question are outcrops of basalt where I stand and get a titillating sense of vertigo at the thought of tripping and plummeting to the valley floor and certain death. But I haven't plummeted yet. My caringness, you see, extends even unto myself.

At the bottom of the hill where the track meets the road there's another bluff. It's a man-made thing in the form of a retaining wall, and if I were to trip over the edge of this bluff I would plummet to a certain sprained ankle. For the wall is 4 feet tall.

But even though this bluff is the lowest on the track by a factor of twenty, a deeply caring protective barrier has recently been erected across its top. The barrier is built of swimming pool fencing. This is apt, because the swimming pool fencing act is one of the most caring pieces of legislation to emerge from Wellington for many a long while. I keenly await its sequel, the sea, river, lake, pond, creek, puddle, bath, basin and dog's water bowl fencing act.

But how do I know that this barrier is a caring barrier? Because it says so. Across the top of it there's a strip of the sort of tape that policemen use to cordon off an accident scene. But this tape does not say 'Accident' on it, or 'Keep Out unless you're an important shaven-headed detective'. This tape says 'City Care'.

Not 'City Maintenance Department'. Not 'Ministry of Works'. Not 'Dirty Municipal Jobs Inc'. But 'City Care'.

Presumably the people who work for City Care are selected for caringness. Not, how big are your biceps, o labourer, but how wide is your heart? I wish I'd seen the wide-hearted ones erecting this barrier, cooing to the 4-inch nails before easing them into place with care and a 16-ounce claw hammer.

Time was when nobody cared. In my youth, for example, if you didn't have a mother or father you had a guardian. That name told you all you needed to know. Guardians were the callous overlords of Dickensian orphanages. When not beating their charges' backsides into biltong, they were sieving the fortnightly gruel ration to remove any traces of nutrition. But that was then and this is now. Guardians are gone and in their place have come caregivers. Indeed, since it is not all that long ago that I was a youth, it is just possible that some of yesterday's guardians are today's caregivers. The same people, but oh what a change of heart. Now they enwrap their little charges in the warm duvet of care.

Consider medicine. It used to be an inhuman business of science and pills and knowledge, the doctor a remote brute, his treatment mechanistic. But not any more. Medicine's become healthcare. The name implies sugar on every pill and an attitude like melted toffee. While the surgeon saws through your thigh-bone he plays a CD of Simon and Garfunkel.

And only the other day I saw the caring Stephanie 'Steve' Chadwick on television, promoting her caring act of parliament that banishes smokers from pubs. She insisted that smokers were poor people who needed help. She cared, you see. What's more she had overwhelming support from what she called healthcare practitioners, among whom she included herself. For 'Steve' is a midwife.

Picture a midwife and you may see a crone with a face like a boot sole hauling out the new-born, slapping it into life and then rattling grimly off on her black bicycle to the next haulage operation. But not any more. 'Steve' and her caring colleagues now praction healthcare and the name tells us that everything is different. Words are all. Change the name of something and, hey presto, you change the thing itself. Now doctors care, guardians care, labourers care. Their names guarantee it.

Though at the same time I can't help recalling a pop group that went by the name of The Grateful Dead. A year or two ago the leader of The Grateful Dead died. A sorrowful spokesman announced that the surviving members of The Grateful Dead were, and I quote, devastated.

Poor things. I hope someone cared for them.

Sub specie aeternibloodytatis

Let's hypothesise. Let's suppose for one moment that you have come home from the pub on the night when the smoking ban came into force. Yes, *that* smoking ban, the one that defies every rational, moral, social and economic argument, the one that depends on the demonisation of a minority in a manner that would have made Hitler's heart swell.

You left the pub shortly before the hour when every publican in the land was required by law, on his own private premises, to throw away his ashtrays and to declare himself 'smokefree', as if he and his business had been born again and would henceforth be a shining light of virtue in the halls of righteousness. And let's suppose, just for the sake of it, that in addition to being angry at the deception and the bullying foisted upon you and your society, you are drunkish.

The dogs greet your return with the sort of joyous abandon that you doubt you will ever achieve again, having been deprived by grinning puritans of the pub, your one remaining source of social stimulation. You frolic as best you can with the dogs, but you do not find it easy. You are consumed with an image of the world that the puritans are trying to create, a world as sterile as an operating ward, a joyless world in which television newsreaders are stars and in which it is your duty to live so long that your mind goes walkabout and you are left by a rest home window to watch the sun crawling across the sky for twenty-five uncomprehending years. A sort of California. A sort of air-conditioned nirvana where the dominant emotion is fear and the dominant activity is shopping.

Your mood, in other words, is sombre. Nor is it lightened by the thought that as a smoker you have become a leper, someone deserving of pity but at the same time ostracised, an unclean thing. Furthermore, the taxes on your cigarettes will pay the salaries of the very people who gave you leprosy. What can you do? You feel impotent, fist-clenchingly bitter. The dogs, however, are looking at you with the eyes of optimists and you decide yes, even if you can no longer feel joy yourself, you can still give joy to others.

For a while, anyway. Because with the puritans at the wheel it is only a matter of time before dog-owning becomes as tightly circum-scribed by law as smoking. Similar fallacious emotive arguments will be used to convince the gullible and timid masses that dogs, in defiance of all evidence, are another threat to their well-being. Soon 'Dogfree' signs will start popping up around parks, neighbourhoods, whole timorous townships. So, 'Come on, dogs,' you say, 'we're going out.'

It is midnight. It is drizzling. You don't mind. Indeed, you barely notice. Up the hill you go, your two black dogs dissolving into the night to become occasional snatches of noise, a swish of tail against grass stems, a swoosh of undergrowth. Near the top of the track you step over a fence and wade through thigh-deep grass, the front of your trousers growing heavy with absorbed water, your mood lightening a little with the exercise and with pleasure in the dogs' pleasure. Then you reach the crest of a long and seriously steep slope.

You have clambered down this slope many times, but never at midnight and never in the rain and never drunk. You toy briefly with the notion of going back the way you came, dismiss it on the principle that it is always better to advance than to retreat, and you step off the edge. Your left foot slithers from under you and you land on your back. As you try to break your fall you grab blindly at a thistle and a thousand tiny prickles lodge in your skin. You are lying in wet vegetation. There is a hundred metres of vertiginousness between you and the track home. You are cold, you are wet and there's a smoking ban. What to do? Easy. Swear.

Swear hugely and loudly to the inky sky. Top-of-the-voice stuff. Let it all go. Pick the vocabulary of your choice and give it to the sky with every millilitre of breath that smoking has left you with. Having got that out of the way, take a look at yourself *sub specie aeternitatis*, a poor wet forked animal on a random hill with a random brace of dogs and with two-thirds of your life behind you. Take in the black and broody hills, the immensity of the world's indifference, the absurdity of striving, and laugh. Laugh as loudly as you swore, with all the gusto you can manage. Think of the puritans and laugh louder.

Your swearing done, your laughing done, set yourself a challenge. Say that you are going to get down this hill come what may, and that you will do so without falling more than twenty-five times in the process. Then get up and go.

It works, I promise. When I reached the track home I was drenched, sore and bleeding but my mood was as light as thistle-down. And I had three falls to spare.

Entropic cookery

Stew's a breeze.

The first thing you need is cheap meat. Get a lot of it and cut it up. But be sure to avoid offal. The Scots get it right. With an accuracy that is frankly atypical, they pronounce offal the same way as they pronounce awful.

The school I attended regularly served liver for lunch. It came in curling slices the colour of asphalt and it landed on your plate with a small but perceptible bounce. Only one child regularly ate it. His name was Doxton. Doxton also ate pens and, if you offered him cash, flies.

The school's reason for serving liver was that it was cheap. The school's excuse for serving liver was that it was good for children. Liver contained iron. So did the hinges on our desks. Admittedly Doxton never suffered anaemia. But he did suffer ostracism.

Anyway, apart from offal, all meat is fine for a stew. The same is more or less true of vegetables. Just steer clear of the green ones. They are the horticultural equivalent of liver. Otherwise pretty well any vegetables that came out on the ground will do. (If they grew above ground keep them for dessert. Only don't call it dessert. Goulash is followed by dessert. Stew is followed by pudding. The difference between stew and goulash is pretension. The difference between pudding and dessert is size.)

The quality and age of the vegetables are immaterial. Onions with a crown of shoots, carrots you can knot, mushrooms with skin like old people's hands – all these are dandy. Just cut them up. If you want to use fancy vegetables like yams, or zucchini (are these green?), or aubergines the size and shape of a bull's testicles, go ahead. They may make a difference. I wouldn't know. But the base rule of stew is that cheapest is best.

Except for the onions, don't peel the vegetables. Their skin is nutritious. And peeling a potato expends more energy than is left in the potato. Whether you wipe the dirt from the potato before chopping it is a matter of personal taste.

How you chop the vegetables up doesn't matter either, except with the carrots. Never dice carrots. Diced carrots are depression on a plate. They taste of institutions where the uniform has buckles at the back.

So, you've got a pile of meat bits and a pile of vegetable bits. Well done. You're almost there. Now fetch a crock pot. A crock pot is like the offspring of Jesus and a tortoise. It works miracles but slowly.

Bung the meat and vegetables into the crock pot. Tip in some water but not much. Meat and vegetables seem to produce their own water. Don't ask me how. Whatever you do, don't add wine, beer, port, brandy or anything else that's better drunk. Drink it. Booze in the stew doesn't make the stew taste nicer. Booze in the cook does.

Now is the time for the creative bit, the sort of activity that makes television chefs rich. Add stuff. The stuff you add is in your cupboard. It's the stuff you bought packets of when you got sucked in by a television chef. Or else it was left behind by the niece who came to stay and thanked you by cooking tajine of Mongolian lamb with coriander and cumin on the last night instead of going to the pub.

Put in lots of everything. Mixed herbs, tomato sauce, curry powder, chilli powder, gravy browning, bay leaves, anything, in short, that's in the food cupboard but that isn't actually food. Stock powder is good. It doesn't matter what kind. If you've got several kinds, use them all. The correct quantity to add of everything is as much as you like. Few of the things will make any difference. But do include flour. It turns the stew into something that labels on cans of soup call hearty. This means it has the texture of wallpaper paste.

Then the fun part. Put the lid on the crock pot and go away. If, when you come back, nothing has happened, you haven't been away long enough. Or else you haven't turned the crock pot on. If the former, go away again. If the latter, turn it on, then go away again.

How long should you stay away? Well, one day's good, two days are better. The aim of the exercise is entropy. If you can still recognise the ingredients, the stew isn't stew. It's soup. Soup's good but stew's excellent. A stew is a fusion, a melding, a mess, a pottage. A pottage takes time.

Prepare to serve the stew by drinking. Then drink some more. If you've got guests turn the stew into a casserole. This is done by ladling it into a posh dish. To turn it into goulash you can add red stuff. Tomato paste works well. Or else give the guests even more to drink then just tell them it's goulash.

But the best way to eat stew is alone with a dog. Dole the stuff onto two plates and offer the dog a race. The dog will win but that's good for your humility. And the dog will ask for seconds, which is good for your pride. And if you've drunk enough and eaten the stew fast enough, you won't taste it.

O'Fishal and Poon

In the early 1970s a save-the-whale demonstration took place in my home town. A friend and I went along to stage a brief two-man counter-demonstration under a placard that we thought was terribly funny. It read 'What about the plankton?' A gentleman with a beard and biceps did not agree that our placard was terribly funny which explains the brevity of our counter-demonstration.

I mention this event not only to establish my credentials in environmental matters, but also to explain my presence at a fishing industry beano in Tokyo last month. I had been flown there as an independent observer courtesy of Hypothetical Airlines. And it so happened that this was the beano at which officials from the New Zealand Ministry of Fisheries allegedly ate whale meat.

The story shocked and staggered the conservation community. Shocked Greenpeace spokespeople staggered out of their community in order to express their staggering shockedness to every news organisation in the land. 'We're shocked and staggered by what happened at the Tokyo beano,' they said.

Fortunately I was there and heard it all. Even more fortunately I was wearing a miniature tape-recorder concealed in my WWF badge. The following is a transcript of the tape. Three people can be heard: a

Japanese fishing magnate called Mr Poon; a smouldering anonymous geisha girl whose job it is to inveigle foreign fisheries officials into compromising situations vis-à-vis forbidden fruits de mer; and a functionary from the New Zealand Ministry of Fisheries who cannot be named for legal reasons and whom I shall call O'Fishal. The action takes place over a glass of sake in a downtown Tokyo fish joint.

Poon: Hello Mr O'Fishal, and welcome to Japan.

O'Fishal: Hello Mr Poon.

Poon: My friends call me Ha.

O'Fishal: Rightio, Ha. (Raising sake glass in universal gesture of international co-operation and a desire to get drunk at taxpayers' expense.) Banzai.

Poon: Bottoms up. Oh look, here comes a smouldering anonymous geisha girl whose job it is to inveigle foreign fisheries o… whoops. Tell me, smouldering anonymous geisha girl, do you have any sumptuous marine morsels with which to tickle the palate of Mr O'Fishal, my new friend from New Zealand? (As he speaks he delivers a monstrous stage wink to the smouldering anonymous geisha girl, hereinafter SAGG.)

SAGG: Certainly Mr Poon. (She unclips a fold of her kimono to reveal a platter of sushi.) Please help yourself, Mr O'Fishal.

O'Fishal:. Don't mind if I do. (Chews appreciatively.) Mmmm, delicious. I'm sorry, what was your name again?

Poon: Ha ha ha.

O'Fishal: Of course. Well, Ha, this really is frightfully…

Poon: Ha ha ha.

O'Fishal: I'm sorry?

Poon: Ha ha ha. You're eating whale, O'Fishal. Humpback to be precise.

O'Fishal (shocked and staggering): I'm shocked and staggered. O Mr Ha, o smouldering anonymous geisha, I don't understand how you can eat whale meat.

Poon: Well, you do have to chew on the blubbery bits for a while, but if you marinade it in …

O'Fishal: No, I mean, in New Zealand we don't eat whales.

Poon: What do you do with them?

O'Fishal: We watch them.

Poon: We watch them in Japan too. Otherwise people nick them.

O'Fishal: No no, you don't understand. We pay people to take us out to sea on boats or small noisy aeroplanes and we wait for a whale to come up for breath and then the boats and the aeroplanes all rush towards it and then …

Poon and SAGG in unison: Yes?

O'Fishal: Then we watch it.

Poon: You watch it.

O'Fishal: Yes.

Poon: What does it do?

O'Fishal: Nothing much. It just breathes a bit, I suppose.

Poon: And you watch it breathing.

O'Fishal: Yes.

Poon: Why?

O'Fishal: Whales are big and they're nice.

Poon: So, in New Zealand you enjoy watching nice big things breathe. Do you also go and watch cows breathe? Tell me Mr O'Fishal, what's the difference between a cow and a whale?

O'Fishal: Mmmm …

Poon: Well, I wouldn't send you to do the milking. Ha ha ha.

SAGG: Oh, very funny, Mr Poon. Ha ha ha.

O'Fishal: But whales are rare. Cows aren't rare. There are lots and lots of cows.

Poon: I see. So you enjoy watching rare things breathe. Then tell me, Mr O'Fishal, do you go on expeditions to find the extremely rare carnivorous snail of Taranaki and then stand around watching that breathe, too?

O'Fishal: Well, no, but …

Poon: Or rare sea urchins, or algae or earthworms? Or are these things not big enough and nice enough to be watched? It seems to me, O'Fishal, my friend, that you are inconsistent and sentimental. Was it not an English-speaking poet who wrote:

He prayeth best that loveth best
All things both great and small.
The streptococcus is the test,
I love him best of all.

In other words, Mr O'Fishal, what about the plankton?

Nesting recruits

Friends of mine have just bought a house, poor darlings. I like them but I can't say that I like the house. Well, actually, I can say that I like the house. Indeed I have said that I like the house. I've said it several times and straight to their faces.

Were I a remotely honest man I would have said that the house was never a pretty thing and that anyway it had been buggered around beyond redemption by the previous owner. Someone had clearly given this man a hammer and chisel set for Christmas, and The Big Cheese, who is always fond of a practical joke, had chipped in by endowing him with an undissuadable belief in both his aesthetic judgement and his talent for carpentry. The results litter the house in the form of chipboard shelves, an abundance of cupboards and a fence round the backyard that would baffle Escher. But have I said so? Of course I haven't. 'What a nice house,' I've said, and the new owners have gulped down the fib like starving Labradors. For one's first house is like one's first child.

They've got one of those too, only a month or two into its journey down the years, poor thing, and I can't say I've been completely frank about that either. The little critter's got about as much hair as I have, and a similarly battered-looking face, but that's where the resemblance ends. I'm as hungry for attention as the next man, but if you ignore me for three nano-seconds I don't crumple my face like a ball of wastepaper, writhe, bunch my fists, gather all my puny force into my lungs and emit a wail so potent that it would guide ships to safety in fog. That wail acts on every woman within a hundred yards in the same way as pheromones act on moths. Up to the cot they sprint like iron filings to a magnet, squabbling over the right to pick up and console the wizened little thing and offer it a one-sided conversation that begins with there there, moves through a forest of diddums, sweetypies and coochycoos and concludes with my departure in search of a bucket. Meanwhile the loveable little ball of wrinkles keeps the noise up for a bit, probably out of some instinctive presentiment that it's never going to have things this easy again. It's in the same position as a novice skier who's just been up the chairlift for the first time. With shaking knees the skier surveys the world and discovers that there's nothing ahead of him except seventy years of downhill horror.

And it's not just for junior that the future's downhill. Mumsy and Dadsy are rocketing in the same direction at a speed that's frankly appalling. Hitherto they've been rootless, profligate and very good fun, but now that they're building a nest those days are emphatically over. And roughly 50 per cent of them seem happy about it.

So are 100 per cent of their married friends, because these new recruits to the nesting classes have provided the old hands with the chance to get rid of stuff. A Niagara of unwanted and unwantable stuff is tumbling into the house from garages and lock-ups and spare bedrooms the length and breadth of Lyttelton.

It's a sort of reverse burglary. Everything that's cluttering up the houses of the established is being palmed off on the beginners. You should see the stuff. First came the furniture, tip-fodder every bit of it, broken-backed gloom upholstered in draylon, singing a song of suburban consumption that would make Leonard Cohen sound merry. And then came the other stuff, the small stuff. Teapots in the shape of chickens, spice racks, bent cutlery. Only this morning when I went round on request to bang a few 4-inch nails into the broken leg of a fifth-hand slat bed, a woman showed up at the house with a cardboard box. Inside the box was a fondue set with a flower pattern round its rim so indescribable that I'm not going to describe it. 'Can't bear to think of you trying to get by without one of these,' she said, more or less, then left at the speed of a city councillor leaving the back door of a brothel. Much of the stuff has already gone straight to the back of the DIY cupboards – God, you should see those cupboards, the design of them, the size of them, the sheer number of them – from which it will emerge only when some other poor sods get hitched and housed and sprogged, and my friends, now wise in the business of ownership, see the chance to pass it all on.

It's all too dreary to contemplate. I rang just now to see if hubby wanted to go for a possum hunt on the hills with the dogs and he said sorry, no, he was going, oh crikey dick, to Placemakers. To buy tools. It's all over. Ah well.

Bloody Wednesday

Bloody Wednesday began at six in the evening. I was going out.

Because I was going out I was shaving. Because I was shaving I was showering. Because I was showering I was singing. Because I was singing I was waving my arms. And because I was waving my arms I cut myself. The razor took a sliver of skin from the base of my left nostril. There was no pain. There was only blood. The blood was a pain.

In general I suppose one should be grateful for bleeding. It's a worrying business but not half so worrying as not bleeding. At the time, however, I didn't think that way. I knew only that a public display of blood was indecent.

I don't know what the coagulant things that haemophiliacs haven't got are called but I addressed them as antibodies. 'Come on antibodies,' I said, 'go to it. I've got to go out. With an editor. You can't bleed before an editor.' But the antibodies refused to go to it. Perhaps I'd misaddressed them.

The quantity of blood bore no relation to the size of the wound. Withdrawing the wad of Kleenex revealed a nick with the girth of an ant's leg. Momentarily it would be clean and white-edged and innocuous, but then it would ooze. It oozed disproportionately.

Blood dripped to the bathroom floor where my larger and keener dog licked at it.

In the bathroom cabinet I found a stick of stuff that claimed to stem the flow of shaving nicks. I was required to moisten the stick then dab it. I moistened and dabbed. The stick spread the blood around nicely but its only significant effect was to increase the flow.

It is hard to put on trousers while one hand is clamping Kleenex to a nostril. It is even harder to put on a shirt, and harder still to take a shirt off again because you've smeared blood on the collar.

When the taxi turned into the drive I ran back to the bathroom cabinet. Mine is not a well-stocked bathroom cabinet. Its aggregate total of sticking plasters stood at one. To describe that single plaster as bright orange would be to understate it. It was funky fluorescent orange.

A nostril is a hard spot to plaster. I stuck the thing diagonally from cheek to top lip. 'What you do to face?' asked the taxi driver who was Korean and amused. 'You should see the other bloke,' I said. 'Eh?' said the driver. I said nothing. I was concentrating on calm, hoping to slow my fluttering heart, to reduce blood pressure, to render my circulation sluggish and my appearance socially acceptable.

Once upon a time people didn't mind the sight of blood. They thought war was noble, and their sort of war meant blood by the bucketful. There was none of this cruising at 30,000 feet and pinging a laser-guided missile between the horns of your enemy's helmet and recording the lot on grainy night-vision TV for the delectation of a billion sitting rooms. No, war was more like a form of pig-sticking in which the pig had a stick as well. So any ancient who made it to manhood was familiar with hacking limbs off and seeing the arterial stuff come pumping from the severed thigh or shoulder like one of those fountain displays that civic leaders are fond of erecting in memory of themselves.

The Romans in particular were steeped in blood. They practised an amusing little pastime called the blood eagle in which the ambition was to slice through the sternum of the enemy, open the rib cage like a kitchen cupboard and pluck the heart from its shelf while it was still beating. The victor then held the heart aloft and went whatever the Latin is for bingo. Our Latin teacher used to mime the activity on the unfortunate Mahoney who struggled appallingly with the subjunctive. In a form of revenge, old JB would flatten Mahoney over the desk and unzip his sternum with the board rubber while Mahoney squealed with terror, and we, caring and sympathetic as all thirteen-year-old boys are, squealed with delight. I sometimes think of Mahoney. I'd love to know his ward number.

But the modern world is less comfortable with blood than the earthier ancient world. To bleed publicly today is bad form. It is unseemly. And so is an orange sticking plaster on the face.

Getting out of the taxi I unpeeled the plaster with the caution of a surgeon. The antibodies seemed finally to have come to the party and I went to mine. It was a lovely evening. The editor poured beer and flattery down me and I drank deeply of both.

When I got home I was a little unsteady, presumably from loss of blood. The dogs greeted me with their standard exuberance. Bending to pat one I overbalanced. I chose to break my fall by applying my ear to the edge of the door. Blood welled. I went in search of a sticking plaster. My aggregate total of sticking plasters stood at none. I went to bed and bled, with no one to see but the dogs. And they didn't mind.

Dead honest

Hilaire Belloc was a fat poet with an odd name. I expect he would deny that his name was odd, but he's dead so he won't.

Belloc wrote some good kiddies' poems and a few, a very few, excellent proper poems. The best of these are short. Among them is one that I am fond of without ever quite understanding it.

I said to heart, 'How goes it?' Heart replied,
'Right as a ribstone pippin,' but it lied.

The poem seems to say something true, but all I can tell you for sure about it is that a ribstone pippin is an apple.

There is another Belloc poem that is preoccupying me at the moment, however, one that keeps sounding in my head to the rhythm of my feet when I'm out on the hills with the dogs and the sky, and it's an easier poem to understand.

I'm tired of love; I'm still more tired of rhyme.
But money gives me pleasure all the time.

A poet is not supposed to say stuff like that. A poet is supposed to live in a garret with love, rhyme, wild hair and empty pockets. That image is a legacy of romanticism and like most romanticism it is nonsense. Roy Fuller, who was always a respectable poet and sometimes a good one, was chairman of the Woolwich Building Society. T. S. Eliot worked in a bank.

The demonic Dylan Thomas, who traded on the poetic image and took care to die disgracefully and young, never worked in a bank, but he was deeply fond of cash. He kept borrowing it from friends, which proves that he preferred it to them.

Today I bought a house. I don't like it much but it comes with two goats that I do like. In order to pay for the house and goats I have had to gather my money. Over recent years I've buried bits of money in funds and bank accounts. Putting the money in was easy. Getting it out has been hard.

One fund said they would need ten working days to find my money. When those days were up I rang to ask where the dosh was. They said they hadn't received a form that I had to sign. I said that they hadn't sent me a form to sign. 'Oh dear,' they said. 'Sorry about that. We'll send it immediately.' I said I needed the money now to buy goats. They said it couldn't be done inside another ten working days. I grew heated. I got my money in the end but I had to swear for it.

When I say my money, I mean what was left of my money. The fund had generated a lot of paper. I had received countless glossy magazines saying what a cracking fund it was. What the fund hadn't generated was profit.

The glossy magazines contained a lot of photographs of men in suits. Most were as fat as Belloc and all were smiling. They were smiling because they were not losing money. They never lose money. When you put the money into their fund they take a cut. When you take it out they take a cut. And when they're looking after it, whether the money swells or shrinks, they take a cut. That's a lot of cutting.

It is easy to dislike money men. They have always had a bad press.

But there has never been any shortage of people willing to be money men, because dealing in money seems to be the best way to make the stuff. But somehow it seems wrong.

Yesterday in a supermarket car park a woman said hello. I didn't remember her. She told me I had taught her son and she named him. I remembered the son. He was a splendid kid. He laughed a lot, worked hard at stuff that mattered, disdained stuff that didn't matter, and was kind of heart.

'What's he up to?' I asked.

'Gone to Sydney,' said his mother, 'and doing well. I don't understand exactly what he does, but basically he trades in money.'

'Oh,' I said and I bit back the words I wanted to say because she was his mother.

Here was a lad I'd liked. In third form English he had written clumsy poems. In seventh form English he had admired the less clumsy poems that I suggested he should admire. He had seemed, in short, as right as a ribstone pippin. And now he was trading money. No doubt he was earning heaps. No doubt he was good at it. But something near instinctive inside me delivered a jolt of disappointment. I felt that somehow he'd sold out.

And yet this morning, just before I paid for my goats and the house that came with them, I had a mass of money in my account, more than I had ever held before. I logged onto my bank on the Internet and I stared at the money. It was mine. It felt fat and good. It gave me pleasure.

Am I a hypocrite? Am I self-deluding? I think Belloc would say so. But he's dead so he won't.

Surprise, Sir Clive

What made the Lions test such an exciting prospect was that we had been told to expect surprises. Would coach Henry deliver those surprises or would coach Woodward? The answer was as obvious as it was arboreal. Woodward would.

Thus far on tour the British and Irish Lions had played indifferent rugby. In the test match we all expected them to play differently. But by the same token, if they did play differently it would not be a surprise, so they chose to continue to play indifferently. Sir Clive is remarkably subtle.

There were abundant individual surprises as well. Gavin Henson, for example, has been in surprise mode from the start of the tour. He emerged from a Welsh winter with a tan like a Moroccan summer. He was also such an obvious shoo-in for the test team that surprisemeister Woodward dropped him. Henson was so surprised his hair stood on end.

The Welsh had surprised everybody by winning the Six Nations tournament. Woodward then surprised the Welsh by leaving most of them out of the Lions. Instead, he toured the knacker's yard and collected the old war horses who had surprisingly won the World Cup for England. To everyone's surprise they looked knackered.

Scotland had not won the World Cup. In the Six Nations they beat only Italy. As a result I half expected Sir Clive to favour them for the Lions, but again Sir Clive surprised by not surprising. He picked no Picts.

And that was not the end of the surprises. By halfway through the second half of the test, O'Driscoll had been stretchered off, O'Connell sent off and Byrne subbed off. Thus in little more than an hour Woodward had surprisingly achieved what centuries of British governments had longed to achieve: he'd entirely got rid of the Irish. So the British and Irish Lions became the English and a few Welsh Lions. Surprisingly they didn't play any better.

Jason Robinson, the Lions fullback, is a surprising runner. He begins every run with a static stutter as if he were typing a letter with his feet. It's a short letter but an effective tactic. The opposition tends to pull up as if to read the letter, whereupon Robinson zings the carriage return and sprints off sideways in his typing boots. But cunning Sir Clive realised that after many seasons of success this technique had lost its element of surprise, so he instructed Robinson to surprise the All Blacks by kicking the ball. He did this badly, which came as a surprise to no one except Robinson and Woodward.

One surprise that surprised everybody was the Lions' decision not to jump in the line-outs. The All Blacks were clearly surprised but managed to overcome their surprise sufficiently to score a try from a line-out. The Lions seemed surprised, but this was probably just a ruse.

It is hard to wring a surprise out of Jonny Wilkinson. Jonny is so marvellously straight. His nose is straight, his devotion unswerving and his manner so earnest you could call it Hemingway. Jonny would have served admirably in the First World War. He would have saluted Captain Clive, led his men over the top and been shot and decorated in that order.

Nevertheless Sir Clive managed to spring a Wilkinson surprise. Instead of playing him in the position in which he wins games for

England, he played him in the position in which Henson wins games for Wales.

When Jonny heard that he was playing in an unfamiliar position, his hair did not stand on end. Instead he loyally insisted that he wasn't at all surprised and that the unfamiliar position was perfectly familiar and was called, well he couldn't quite remember what it was called, but it was an honour to play there for the surprising Sir Clive. He then played there honourably.

The only familiar position Jonny found himself in was the one he adopts to take penalties. He resembles an anxious tourist squatting over an untouchable foreign lavatory. But for once, and surprisingly, Jonny's kicks weren't as straight as the kicker.

The Lions, then, were crammed with surprises, but the French ref did his bit too. When he spoke he didn't sound like a Frenchman speaking English. He sounded like Peter Sellers impersonating a Frenchman speaking English. Even more surprisingly he proved a competent referee.

The All Blacks also had a surprise or two up the sleeves of their sleeveless shirts. The best of their surprises was occasionally to give the Lions the ball. The Lions were so surprised they passed it behind each other or dropped it. Eventually, however, the Lions overcame their surprise and learned to kick the ball back to the All Blacks.

In short, then, the test match turned out exactly as everyone had expected it to, which was something of a surprise.

Keep 'em poor

Make poverty history, scream the ageing rock stars. Are they out of their minds?

Well, of course they're out of their minds. They're ageing rock stars. Their minds were addled in adolescence by adulation and acid, and re-addled in middle age by knighthoods. But that barely excuses the banality of their thinking. Making poverty history would be disastrous.

Who'd manufacture my underpants, my training shoes, my dehumidifier or the combined key-fob, penlight and nail clipper that I picked up for a song at The Warehouse the other day and that has afforded me such delight? No, sharing out the global goodies sounds all nice and sugary, but when underpants hit the sort of prices that only Tuku Morgan's prepared to pay then the sugar will start to taste rancid. The rich world needs poverty.

Consider golf. At present you can get onto a golfcourse with reasonable ease everywhere but Japan. There may be a bit of a queue on a Sunday morning, but it's no great suffering to hang around in a pair of ghastly Chinese slacks and polo shirt, toying with your Indian-made Pings amid surroundings rendered pleasant by the sort of people who can't afford to belong to the club. Make poverty history, however, and not only would you have to mow your own fairways but you wouldn't be able to get into the clubhouse for the pullulating hordes from Delhi and Darfur waving their newly acquired dollars above their heads, yelling for gin and haggling over the bar prices as if it was some sort of Moroccan street market because they hadn't yet had a century or two of swaddled prosperity to teach them manners. No, it's unthinkable, catastrophic in every way.

The tourism industry would shrivel like the before shot in a Viagra ad. I mean, bung a few dollars into the hands of the deprived and however vigorously you flourish your platinum Amex card outside Dar es Salaam railway station, you won't be able to find a porter. The locals are absolutely charming at present of course because we've got the dosh. But toss them a bit of prosperity and see what happens to those welcoming smiles and garlands of flowers at the airport. Precisely. They'd melt faster than the morning mist over a lump of gorilla-infested jungle in Zaire. Furthermore you wouldn't find locals with an Incentive Saver account hanging around in decorative little huts doing picturesque peasanty things with oxen and pre-industrial agricultural machinery for us to point the Nikon at. No, they'd be razing the gorilla-infested jungle and erecting the African equivalent of Fendalton before you could say embryonic real estate industry. And who's going to go on safari to Fendalton?

Not of course that there'd be anything left to go on safari for. The first thing the newly enriched would do would be exactly what we did when we first started squirrelling the stuff away in bank accounts, which was to eliminate all environmental threats to our well-being. Kalashnikov sales would go through the roof and that would be that for tigers, rhinos, snakes and all the rest of the excitingly nasty bits of nature that we haven't got any more but that we're keen for them to keep. That croc-wrestling Aussie, for example, the one with the shorts and the fake enthusiasm and the billion-decibel whisper, would be out of a job overnight. Nothing to lament in his demise, of course, but with him would go an entire industry that exists purely to indulge and amuse us fatsos in the West, to wit the animal porn business featuring regal predators and rather less regal herbivores being hauled down and having their jugulars punctured for us to enjoy in super slow-mo. All gone. David Attenborough on the dole and the Natural History channel showing either static or documentaries about Cruftos, the Amazon poodle show. Curtains too for *National Geographic* magazine, taking with it a whole tradition of sagging African breasts and closet pre-teen pleasure. And that's just the entertainment side of global poverty.

Start thinking resources and you realise the full insanity of the naïve proposals of that Irish rocker who's named after a dog-biscuit. Already, as a result of a mere decade selling underpants, socks and All Black regalia to the West, a few million Chinese have started on the long march to Prosperityville and look what's happened to the price of steel. And have you tried to buy a tonne of copper ore recently? Nor have I as it happens, but apparently the stuff's all headed for Shanghai as fast as they can shovel it out of the ground. As for oil, well, there's precious little left as it is, and if every pauper round the globe got his work-callused mitts on a rusting Corolla it would be $500 a barrel within minutes. Not to mention the pollution which it is our job to produce and theirs to endure the consequences of. Though of course the newly rich would refuse to endure the consequences of it any more, and as global warming rendered everything within a thousand miles of the equator uninhabitable, where would they all be heading next, eh? To war, that's where.

So what are the rockers on about? It's tempting to imagine that it's all a ruse to induce the Third World to forsake its awful traditional music and buy some even more awful rock music. But the rock stars can't be that clever, surely.

Fifty thousand an hour, money-makingly

'O Harry,' said Hermione introductorily, 'I've got this cracking idea for a new plot.'

'Good,' said Harry Potter. 'About time.'

'Why do you say that?' asked Hermione interrogatively.

'Well,' said Harry, 'according to the text I'm only fourteen, but in real time I'm in my early twenties and after all those scrapes we've been through together, Hermione, I've got to know you really well and, frankly, my wand…'

'O Harry,' interrupted Hermione blush-sparingly, 'you silly beast. Asexuality's a convention of children's literature and so you're going to have to wait till after the final book in the series which probably won't arrive for another year or two. Do you think you can hold on?'

'I'll try,' said Harry leg-crossingly.

'Meanwhile,' said Hermione subject-changingly, 'we need a new plot. Some of the critics have been giving us a bad time. They say the books are clunkily written…'

'What?' interrupted Harry clunkily. 'What do they mean, clunkily?'

'And,' continued Hermione apparently non-Harry-hearingly, 'that the whole of our story is simply a corny battle between good and evil using time-worn cliché-ridden medieval imagery.'

As she spoke a silvery-blue dragon reared coincidentally onto its hind legs, writhing with all its might and spitting fire from its vicious-looking fanged mouth, the sparks raining down on its scaly hide.

'Is that all?' asked Harry.

'By no means,' said Hermione. 'They also say that Hogwarts is parodic nostalgia, a sort of Billy Bunter with magic, and that most of the incidental characters speak like Spitfire pilots in black and white films.'

'Whoa, there,' shouted a moustachioed wizard illustratively as he struggled to restrain the dragon on a stout leather leash, 'just look at her plume of fire. Isn't she a beauty?'

'So what do you say to that, Harry?' asked Hermione point-makingly.

'Fifty thousand copies an hour,' said Harry, 'is what I say to that. We're selling fifty thousand copies an hour. The critics are just ... are just ... help me out, Hermione.'

'Green with envy,' said Hermione outhelpingly.

'Precisely,' said Harry. 'They're just green with envy. But what's your new plot element?'

'Well,' said Hermione well, 'I think we need a new evil character, so I've come up with a German.'

'Oh, now that *is* a good idea,' said Harry. 'That fits in nicely with our air of fifties style Britishness. But what's this character's name? Names are everything in our business. We've got Voldemort, who translates, though no one seems to notice, as "flight of death", we've got the posh romanticism of Hermione, the deliberate irony of the ordinariness of Potter, allied to the royal hint in Harry, the Anglo-Saxon consonantality of Hagrid with its intimations of witchcraft, the straightforward demonology of Griffindor, the black and predatory connotations of Ravenclaw, the comic inversion of Warthogs, the...'

'Ratzinger,' said Hermione papally.

'Crikey,' said Harry, 'that's good and nasty. Tell me more.'

'As I see it,' said Hermione, 'Ratzinger sings to rats. He's got a cellar full of rats and he sings instructions to them whereupon they rush out on murderous errands. It's great colour stuff, all German and efficient and sinister.'

'I like it,' said Harry.

'But at the same time Ratzinger belongs to a worldwide organisation led by a frail old man who suddenly ups and dies. All the club elders then go into a huddle and choose Ratzinger to take over. They announce their decision by sending smoke out of a chimney.'

'That's a bit far-fetched, isn't it?' said Harry. 'Do you think people will swallow it?'

'You bet,' said Hermione wageringly. 'But the best bit's still to come. Ratzinger changes his name to something nice and puts on all this medieval finery and then, guess what.'

'What?' said Harry.

'He denounces us. Effectively he declares war on Hogwarts. He says that the stories of our adventures are "subtle seductions".'

'Subtle!' exclaimed Harry. 'There's nothing subtle about Harry Potter.'

'Ah but,' butted Hermione, 'the whole point is that he's a competitor. His organisation runs doctrinal schools like ours and deals like us with imaginary forces to which it gives powerful names, and it sets great store by ritual incantations, and it dresses up a lot of its pronouncements in a dead language that only insiders can understand, and it reveres a book of ancient pronouncements, many of which, it must be said, are contradictory, but still it's a powerful force, and though the organisation doesn't officially believe in witches and wizards it nevertheless condemns them as dabblers in the occult which it also officially doesn't believe in, though it did once, and...'

'It sounds,' said Harry, 'a pretty mixed-up outfit.'

'But a powerful one,' said Hermione.

'Fifty thousand copies an hour powerful?' asked Harry.

'Of course not,' said Hermione, 'and that's the point. It would love to be fifty thousand copies an hour powerful which is why Ratzinger's having a go at us.'

'Green with envy, then,' said Harry. 'Like all the rest of them.'

A short stack with Ben

I'm in Queenstown but my head's in Idaho. I'm thinking of Ben and the boss-eyed woman and the miserable men. I haven't thought of them for twenty years. The pancakes brought them back.

I'm in a diner. Diners are as American as Cadillacs, but you rarely see them outside America because they are good things. America exports only its bad things. It exports fast food, fat tourists and filthy foreign policy. It exports situation comedies that are as funny as leukaemia. It exports Hollywood fantasies to fuel the dreams of the poor in spirit. It exports television evangelists with wigs and grins. It exports fad diets, theories of management, self-help books and rap. And it wonders why there are parts of the world that despise it.

Until I went there I despised America. When I went there I found more kind and generous people than I had met anywhere else. And I found diners. Every diner had a long counter with stools, and booths along the wall. The moment you sat down you got a glass of iced water and a cup of thin coffee.

The glory of diners was the breakfasts. Steak and eggs, hash browns and sausages, and bacon cooked till it snapped. All was cheap and swift and bountiful and served on plates the size of Wisconsin. I always had the pancakes. They came with whipped butter and a synthetic syrup that they called maple. I would smear ounces of butter between the pancakes, drench the lot in syrup, then carve triple-decker wedges of sopping rich sweetness.

And here, this morning, in Queenstown, I ordered pancakes once again. The syrup smelt authentically inauthentic. And the taste brought with it a gust of memory so strong it almost blew me from my stool.

New Year's Eve 1983 and I awoke in Salt Lake City, Utah, the weird heart of the Mormon world. I had wandered its streets for a couple of days, gawping. But Utah was no place to celebrate New Year's Eve and I hitched north out of town. It took all day to reach Idaho. In the first town beyond the border I dumped my bag at a motel and went in search of New Year's Eve debauch. The town was called, if memory serves, Something Falls. The first shop window I passed had a display of T-shirts. The most prominent said 'Something Falls, Idaho, is not the end of the world, but you can see it from here'.

The town had two bars. One was shut. The other was Herman's Tavern. Next door to Herman's Tavern was Herman's Diner.

In the tavern I found Ben the barman, a boss-eyed woman and a table of miserable men. The men wore check shirts and cat hats and sat in silence.

Ben poured me a beer and asked me what I was doing in Something Falls. I said I was looking for fun on New Year's Eve. When I spoke, the table of miserable men swung slowly round en masse and stared at me as cattle do, their eyes all wide and wondering.

'You sure came to the wrong place,' said Ben.

But it was too late to find another place. I spent that New Year's Eve in Herman's Tavern. I drank pitchers of beer with the miserable men. We barely spoke. I played pool against the boss-eyed woman. One eye aimed north-west, the other south-east. She wore jeans of a size that would be unsellable in any other country. When she bent over the table her backside was like two sacks of cement. She thrashed me.

132

At midnight, bells rang on the radio. No one reacted. Ten minutes later Ben said, 'Happy New Year, everyone.' I said, 'Happy New Year, Ben.' One of the miserable men said, 'Fuck off, Ben.'

A little later I got up to leave. The same miserable man asked me where I was going. 'To bed,' I said. 'Like hell you are,' he said and he drove me in his pick-up truck to a house and we drank more beer in silence.

In the morning the only place open for breakfast was Herman's Diner. The boss-eyed woman was cooking. Ben was stretched out on the counter asleep. I sat two place settings beyond his feet. His brown leather boots had a hole in the sole. I ordered pancakes from the boss-eyed woman, ate them, paid, then hitched out of Something Falls. I've not been back.

But now the taste of pancakes has taken me back, back to a single frail travelling coincidence, an event of no significance. And it seems to me now that for twenty-six years my life was destined briefly to collide with the lives of Ben and the men and the boss-eyed woman, like a railway line leading inexorably to a junction. The junction came. We met. And then it was over. That was that. I left Something Falls and the lines of our lives sped away from each other. It meant nothing and it means nothing. It just was.

Where are they now? Dead or alive? Still moping in Herman's Tavern? Still soaking up Budweiser and playing pool? I'll never know. I don't want to know.

And yet it pleases me to think of them, to wonder once again at the web of chance. And here, now, in a diner on the other side of the world, I find myself smiling with the mild intoxication of the utterly random. It's as sweet as syrup.

Light thickens with dogs

'Light thickens,' said Macbeth one evening. He did a nice line in poetry even when he was about to commit murder. 'Light thickens, and the crow makes wing to the rooky wood. Good things of day begin to droop and drowse,' and so saying he pulled on his boots and headed off into the night to kill a king.

I don't know what Macbeth was like at walking in the dark. If he was anything like me, he was hopeless. If he was anything like my dogs, he was brilliant.

Darkness doesn't seem to trouble dogs. Perhaps it's because they see in black and white, so shades of grey for them are business as usual. And anyway their noses act like eyes.

Our noses don't. We are visual creatures so darkness disables us, which is why, like Macbeth, we associate day with good and night with evil.

Last night, when all the good things of Lyttelton had long since drooped and drowsed or gone to the pub, I drove the dogs to the bays. When I opened the car door, the dogs bounded into the bush as if it were noon. Both dogs are black. They disappeared. They went with the sure-footedness of goats.

I followed with the sure-footedness of a drunk. Though I know these paths well, I stumbled and slipped, and where the bush was dense I went with a hand outstretched before me as if trying to stop traffic.

In compensation for my blindness my other senses grew acute. A pine tree smelt of disinfectant. A branch brushed my arm and my skin reacted as if electrocuted. And I had ears as sharp as Spock's. For a while I tracked the dogs by sound – a twig snapping, the heavy panting of my younger dog – but then the dogs rounded a corner or dropped over a bluff and I was alone.

How weak and little is the light,
All the universe of sight,
Love and delight,
Before the might,
If you love it not, of night.

In town the night has never bothered me. I will amble down the darkest of dark alleys, whistling like a boulevardier in springtime, not caring a fig for the knife-toting ruffians with which any film director would people such a spot. But put me in the wilderness at night, however mild that wilderness might be, and I'm on edge. They say it takes imagination to be scared. If so, then I'm an imaginative man.

I remember as a child walking down a country lane at night and flushing a pheasant. It screeched and rose from right beneath my feet as if fired from a silo. I have often noticed that when a startled bird takes off it spontaneously empties its bowels. When this pheasant took off, so did I.

And I remember taking a party of schoolboys fishing. We camped among trees by the Tekapo River. The fishing was good and when dusk fell I was a mile or two upstream. The trout rose with the moon to suck the day's spent insects from the surface of the pool. The fish were audible. The water shivered like mercury. But the darkness made me clumsy and I caught nothing. Then the fish sank back down and all was silvery and still. As I started the trek back to camp, the stones of the riverbank graunched underfoot. Nameless creatures made moan in the bush.

Moonlight is romantic for a couple, but for this solitary fisherman it felt eerie. I would have liked to sing but didn't dare.

Then in the distance I heard my name called. The kids, who were sixteen years old and urban like me, had long since returned to camp and were concerned that I had not. I called back but I was calling against the breeze. I didn't call again.

It took an hour to walk back. When I reached the camp I met an image as old as mankind. The kids were sitting hunched around a fire, the flames casting giant shifting shadows on the wall of trees. I stepped into the clearing and said 'Hello.' The boys rose like pheasants.

Last night was moonless. On the hillside above me a possum cackled. It's a sound that makes you doubt the beast is vegetarian. Where the scrub had been cleared the grass was thick with frost. It felt and sounded like walking on cornflakes.

On the far side of the water a car's headlights swept around a hillside. Behind it the hills were humped grey silhouettes against the rich ink of the sky. I walked a while then called the dogs. My voice sounded absurdly loud.

My dogs are part-time obedient. I called again. Nothing stirred but the echo of the two short syllables. I became aware of my own breathing.

The cold seeped through the soles of my sandshoes. I thought I would retrace my steps to round a bluff and call again. I turned, stepped out and fell smack over a dog. She had slipped quietly up behind me and had stood there with the patience of nature, waiting for me to acknowledge her, black in the blackness and quite at ease, unable to understand my blindness.

My other dog came panting up the hill. 'Hell is murky,' I said, in echo of Lady Macbeth, and we headed for the lights of home.